# WOMEN, WORK AND WAGES:

## *Equal Pay for Jobs of Equal Value*

Donald J. Treiman and Heidi I. Hartmann
Editors

Committee on Occupational Classification and Analysis
Assembly of Behavioral and Social Sciences
National Research Council

NATIONAL ACADEMY PRESS
Washington, D.C.     1981

National Academy Press   2101 Constitution Avenue, N.W.   Washington, D.C. 20418

NOTICE: The project that is the subject of this report was approved by the Governing Board of the National Research Council, whose members are drawn from the councils of the National Academy of Sciences, the National Academy of Engineering, and the Institute of Medicine. The members of the committee responsible for the report were chosen for their special competences and with regard for appropriate balance.

This report has been reviewed by a group other than the authors according to procedures approved by a Report Review Committee consisting of members of the National Academy of Sciences, the National Academy of Engineering, and the Institute of Medicine.

The National Research Council was established by the National Academy of Sciences in 1916 to associate the broad community of science and technology with the Academy's purposes of furthering knowledge and of advising the federal government. The Council operates in accordance with general policies determined by the Academy under the authority of its congressional charter of 1863, which establishes the Academy as a private, nonprofit, self-governing membership corporation. The Council has become the principal operating agency of both the National Academy of Sciences and the National Academy of Engineering in the conduct of their services to the government, the public, and the scientific and engineering communities. It is administered jointly by both Academies and the Institute of Medicine. The National Academy of Engineering and the Institute of Medicine were established in 1964 and 1970, respectively, under the charter of the National Academy of Sciences.

This report was prepared under contract to the U.S. Equal Employment Opportunity Commission. The report, however, does not necessarily represent the official opinion or policy of the Equal Employment Opportunity Commission or any other agency or official of the federal government.

Library of Congress Catalog Card Number 81-82863

International Standard Book Number 0-309-03177-X

First Printing, August 1981
Second Printing, February 1982
Third Printing, May 1984

Printed in the United States of America

*iii*

# Contents

# Tables
# and
# Figures

# Preface

The Committee on Occupational Classification and Analysis was established by the National Research Council in response to requests for assistance from two agencies of the federal government: the Department of Labor asked for an external assessment of its work in the area of occupational classification, in particular as that work is related to the development of the *Dictionary of Occupational Titles*; and the Equal Employment Opportunity Commission (EEOC) asked for an examination of the issues involved in a "comparable worth" concept of job compensation. Our earlier report (Miller et al., 1980) presented the results of our review for the Department of Labor; this report deals with the issues raised by the EEOC.

The issue of "comparable worth" has joined the ranks of those social controversies about equity that have come to the forefront of public discussion in recent decades. As do many of those controversies, it involves questions about the operation of economic institutions, and advocates of "comparable worth" have called for intervention to redress the inequity they perceive to be embedded in the present situation. In essence, the point made is that, within a given organization, jobs that are equal in their value to the organization ought to be equally compensated, whether or not the work content of those jobs is similar. The impetus for the formulation of the "comparable worth" concept has come primarily from the substantial differences in the types of jobs held by men and by women and from the belief that those traditionally held by women receive lower compensation because they are held by women,

The committee took as its first task a review of what might be called "the state of the question." Early meetings were largely occupied with discussions of whether we were addressing a legitimate question and of how we might establish whether we were. We recognized that we were dealing with topics that have a long history among the concerns of social theorists and that continue to present unresolved problems—that is, the allocation of labor and the allocation of rewards for that labor. But the particular context within which these issues are being raised now is new, and the committee consequently spent considerable time establishing the approach to take. We decided that we had to examine the earnings differentials between men and women and then the operation of the labor market. During this period the staff prepared a number of informal memoranda on topics ranging from international approaches to equal pay for work of equal value to guidelines for improving job evaluation procedures. As we proceeded, it became clear that we needed a thorough review of the features of job evaluation plans in order to assess their relevance to discussions of comparable worth. That review was the substance of our interim report (Treiman, 1979). Very gradually a consensus on what other evidence was pertinent and required review also emerged.

The format of the report reflects this consensus. A major portion of our early discussion focused on whether, in fact, the existing wage rate is a good approximation of the worth of a job. Our ultimate view, as described in Chapter 3 and summarized in Chapter 5, is that the substantial influence of institutional and traditional arrangements makes it impossible to view current wage rates as set solely by the free play of neutral forces operating in an entirely open market, no matter how attractive such a theoretical formulation may be. Our examination of the outcomes—that is, the earnings differentials, reviewed in Chapter 2—and the processes—the arrangements by which workers are allocated and wages are set, covered in Chapter 3—led us to that judgment. Moreover, the widespread use of job evaluation plans as aids in determining wage rates appears to us implicitly to confirm our judgment.

Both of the committee's assignments—the review for the Department of Labor and that for the Equal Employment Opportunity Commission—are relevant to issues that continually arise in the operating decisions of persons charged with making the arrangements by which the conditions of employment are set. Both also are relevant to the theoretical and empirical analyses conducted within the frameworks of several social science disciplines. The members of the committee were selected for the diversity of their experience in facing both aspects of these issues. Several have had extensive experience in formulating and administering personnel policies, in negotiating the structure of union-management agreements, and in other closely related activities. Both their operational expertise and their comprehension of the relationship between operational and theoretical aspects were extraordinarily helpful. Our academic members brought the diverse emphases of their disciplines as well as their technical backgrounds in the analysis of data to bear on our discussions in a way that illuminated key factors.

One member, Ernest McCormick, has prepared a minority report presenting his disagreement with the committee report on two issues. One relates to the committee's conclusions that institutional and traditional arrangements often play a major role in setting current wage rates. The second point of dissent relates to the material covered in Chapter 4. The details of the procedures described by McCormick were presented to the committee on several occasions. It was the committee's decision that no detailed exposition of any job evaluation plan belonged in the final report. We are presenting only the essential principles governing those systems that have been used by American firms, and we refer the reader to our interim report for further details and for references to a number of specific proprietary procedures.

This volume also includes a supplementary statement prepared by one member, Gus Tyler, and endorsed by a second, Mary C. Dunlap. Although both members support the committee's report, they believe that the issue with which the report deals—the comparable worth of jobs within an individual firm—is too narrowly focused to have a major impact on the root causes of pay differentials, which, in their view, involve much broader issues. They recognize, however, that it would not be proper for the report itself to raise these issues.

This has not been an easy report to prepare. I am extremely grateful to the staff, particularly the two editors of the report, Donald J. Treiman and Heidi I. Hartmann, for the quality of their work and for their patience in responding to the diverse requests during the long preliminary period in which the committee was developing the structure of the report. Patricia A. Roos was particularly helpful in seeing to the myriad details involved in the last stages of completing the report. Four other members of the committee staff, Benita A. Anderson, Pamela S. Cain, June Price, and Charles F. Turner, whose work was primarily on our report to the Department of Labor, also contributed in many ways to the creation of this report. And Rose S. Kaufman earned the gratitude of all of us for the skill with which she arranged our meetings and the processing of our innumerable drafts.

I should also like to express my appreciation to the reviewers of earlier drafts of this report. The questions they raised and the points they found troubling helped to reveal where the report had failed to state the committee's intent clearly and enabled us to make necessary revisions. My thanks go, too, to Eugenia Grohman and Christine L. McShane, editors on the staff of the Assembly of Behavioral and Social Sciences, for their major contributions in clarifying the text.

Finally, I come to my fellow committee members. The commitment, perseverance, and patience they devoted to the preparation of this report cannot be adequately acknowledged in a few short words. Their support was unfailing, and it was a great pleasure to me to work with them all.

Ann R. Miller, *Chair*
Committee on Occupational
   Classification and Analysis

# 1 Introduction

At the request of the Equal Employment Opportunity Commission (EEOC), the Committee on Occupational Classification and Analysis undertook a study of the issues involved in measuring the comparability of jobs. What bases—skill, effort, responsibility, tasks—exist for comparing jobs? Can they be adequately measured? Specifically, the committee was charged with assessing formal systems of job evaluation and other methods currently used in the private and public sectors to establish the comparability of jobs and their levels of compensation.[1] The EEOC is concerned with the validity of the principles used to establish compensation—in particular, with whether methods of job analysis and classification currently used are biased by traditional stereotypes or other factors.

The committee undertook its investigation at a time when compensation systems are being intensively questioned, especially by women. The issue of the "comparable worth" of jobs is being raised in complaints, grievances, public discussions, lawsuits, and legislative initiatives. Women who are nurses, librarians, government employees, and clerical workers have assessed their skills and the requirements of their jobs and have argued that their jobs are underpaid relative to jobs of

[1] Job evaluation systems typically are used to order jobs hierarchically on the basis of judgments regarding their relative skill, effort, responsibility, etc., and on this basis to group them for pay purposes. For a description of formal job evaluation systems, see Chapter 4 and also the committee's interim report to the Equal Employment Opportunity Commission (Treiman, 1979).

*1*

comparable worth—that is, jobs requiring similar levels of skill, effort, and responsibility and similar working conditions—that are held mainly by men. For many women, the slogan "equal pay for work of equal value" has replaced the slogan "equal pay for equal work," which is embodied in the Equal Pay Act of 1963. More generally, the issue raised is that of pay equity in a labor market that is highly segregated by sex. While the opportunity to move out of segregated job categories may be welcome to many women, many others, who have invested considerable time in training for their jobs, demand wage adjustment in "women's jobs" rather than opportunities to work in other jobs.

A number of lawsuits have been initiated by women who assert that, because Title VII of the 1964 Civil Rights Act makes discrimination in compensation for employment illegal, jobs of comparable worth are required to be compensated equally and that failure to meet this requirement constitutes discrimination. Some of these lawsuits involve job evaluation systems. Nurses working for the City of Denver, for example, claimed that the classification system used by the city's Career Service Authority to assign jobs to pay classifications was discriminatory. Nursing service directors were grouped, for pay purposes, in a pay class that was 86 percent female (including, for example, beginning nurses and dental hygienists) rather than in a pay class comprised of professional jobs, held mainly by men, that were alleged by the plaintiffs to be of equivalent responsibility (for example, hospital administration officers and directors of environmental health). Of a total of 74 administrative pay classes, in 65 classes all job incumbents were men and in 6 classes all incumbents were women; only 3 of the classes had incumbents of both sexes (Kronstadt, 1978). The nurses lost their case in district court, and their appeal to the U.S. Court of Appeals for the Tenth Circuit was unsuccessful (*Lemons* v. *Denver*).

Librarians, too, have challenged the use of classification systems that result in lower pay for what they regard as jobs with requirements similar to those of other nonteaching positions. In 1971 librarians at the University of California found that they were in the lowest of the university's 25 nonteaching academic pay series and that their salaries were about 25 percent lower than the salaries of those in comparable nonteaching academic positions filled mainly by men (Galloway and Archuleta, 1978). In San Francisco, employees of the city and the county compared the pay rates of classes of jobs held mainly by men with the pay rates of classes of jobs held mainly by women. They found salaries of the jobs held mainly by men to be 74 percent higher than salaries of jobs held mainly by women. When comparisons were restricted to jobs requiring equal education and experience, the salary advantage of the jobs held mainly by men ranged from 21 percent for selected professional jobs (for example, recreation instructor or real property appraiser compared with librarian) to 64 percent for selected clerical jobs (for example, storekeeper compared with clerk typist) (Women Library Workers and the Commission on the Status of Women, 1978).

Some groups have relied on job evaluation systems to support their claims of comparable worth. Examples include a number of cases brought by the International Union of Electrical, Radio and Machine Workers, alleging that electrical manufacturing companies had put jobs held exclusively by women into lower pay grades than jobs held exclusively by men, even when the jobs were judged to be of equal value on the basis of the companies' own job evaluation plans that were used as the principal bases of pay differentiation within the companies (see the discussion in Chapter 3). Similarly, women clerical workers at the University of Northern Iowa filed a complaint because craft workers (primarily men) were paid a premium of 50 percent over the salary range dictated by a job evaluation plan used by the university. Justified by the university as a business necessity to compete in the local labor market, the premium had the effect of paying men more on the average and women less on the average than their jobs were worth according to the university's own criteria (*Christensen* v. *Iowa*).

In the State of Washington, the state government employees' union requested that a study be undertaken, using job evaluation techniques, to compare jobs held mainly by men (for example, traffic guide, construction coordinator, electrician) with those held mainly by women (for example, secretary, clerk typist, nurse practitioner). The study found that for jobs rated equally by the job evaluation system, those held mainly by men were paid 20 percent more on the average than those held mainly by women; the difference occurred largely because the state's pay scales had been developed by using area wage surveys (Remick, 1980). Similar studies, relying on job evaluation techniques, are being carried out to analyze civil service classifications in a number of states.

## CURRENT LEGAL CONTEXT

The status of claims of comparable worth under federal law is at present uncertain. Two major federal laws cover employment discrimination: the Equal Pay Act of 1963 and the Civil Rights Act of 1964. The Equal Pay Act of 1963 (an amendment to the Fair Labor Standards Act) addresses the issue of equal pay for men and women doing equal work. The act describes equal work as that requiring equal skill, effort,

and responsibility being performed under similar working conditions.[2]
Under the Equal Pay Act, job pairs such as janitor and maid, nurse's
aide and orderly, and selector-packer and selector-packer-stacker have
been found to be sufficiently similar as to be considered equal, and
equal pay has been ordered.[3] The word "equal" in this context has
been interpreted to require that the jobs so compared be very similar
in work content.

Title VII of the 1964 Civil Rights Act, as amended, prohibits discrimination because of race, color, religion, sex, or national origin in all
employment practices, including hiring, firing, promotion, compensation, and other terms, privileges, and conditions of employment.[4] The

---

[2] The Equal Pay Act states (29 U.S.C. §206(d)(1)(1970)):

No employer having employees subject to any provisions of this section shall discriminate within any establishment in which such employees are employed, between
employees on the basis of sex by paying wages to employees in such establishment
for equal work on jobs the performance of which requires equal skill, effort and
responsibility, and which are performed under similar working conditions, except
where such payment is made pursuant to (i) a seniority system (ii) a merit system
(iii) a system which measures earnings by quantity or quality of production, or (iv)
a differential based on any other factor other than sex: Provided, that an employer
who is paying a wage rate differential in violation of this subsection shall not in
order to comply with the provisions of this subsection, reduce the wage rate of any
employee.

[3] From June 1964 through the end of fiscal 1977 there were 7,878 compliance actions
involving equal pay, and more than $147 million was found to be owed to more than
253,000 employees. Almost $16 million was found to be owed to 19,382 employees in
1977 alone, and nearly 13,000 employees benefited from $7 million in restored income
(U.S. Department of Labor, Employment Standards Administration, 1978).

[4] Title VII states in part (42 *U.S. Code* S20003-2(h)):

Sec. 703 (a) it shall be an unlawful employment practice for an employer—(l) to
fail or refuse to hire or to discharge any individual, or otherwise to discriminate
against any individual with respect to his compensation, terms, conditions, or
privileges of employment, because of such individual's race, color, religion, sex,
or national origin; or (2) to limit, segregate, or classify his employees or applicants
for employment in any way which would deprive or tend to deprive any individual
of employment opportunities or otherwise adversely affect his status as an employee, because of such individual's race, color, religion, sex, or national origin.

The act covers all private employers of 15 or more persons, labor unions with 15 or
more members, all educational institutions, federal, state, and local governments, employment agencies, and joint labor-management committees that provide apprenticeship
or training. Complaints can be filed by individuals who believe they have been discriminated against or can be initiated by the Equal Employment Opportunity Commission,
the federal agency charged with the enforcement of Title VII.

Equal Pay Act was partially incorporated into Title VII via the Bennett Amendment, which states: "It shall not be an unlawful employment practice under this title for any employer to differentiate upon the basis of sex in determining the amount of the wages or compensation paid or to be paid to employees of such employer if such differentiation is authorized by the provisions of [the Equal Pay Act]." Until a recent Supreme Court decision, the interpretation of this language had been in dispute. Some interpretations had held that jobs being compared to establish claims of pay discrimination against women must meet an Equal Pay Act test of similarity. An alternative interpretation had been that the Bennett Amendment was meant to incorporate only the defenses available to an employer that are enumerated in the Equal Pay Act: that is, if an employer can show that pay differences stem from seniority, merit, differences in productivity, or differences in any factor other than sex, then those differences in pay are not illegal.

In June 1981 the U.S. Supreme Court ruled, in *County of Washington et al.* v. *Gunther et al.* (80-429), in favor of the latter interpretation: "The Bennett Amendment does not restrict Title VII's prohibition of sex-based wage discrimination to claims for equal pay for 'equal work.' Rather, claims for sex-based wage discrimination can also be brought under Title VII even though no member of the opposite sex holds an equal but higher paying job, provided that the challenged wage rate is not exempted under the Equal Pay Act's affirmative defenses as to wage differentials attributable to seniority, merit, quantity or quality of production, or any other factor other than sex" (Syllabus, i–ii).

The Court made no explicit judgment regarding the validity of the concept of comparable worth as a basis for assessing pay equity between jobs, noting that such a judgment was not relevant to the dispute. Despite this, the Court appears to distinguish between cases in which plaintiffs ask the courts to judge the relative worth of jobs and cases in which plaintiffs demand that, where employers have made judgments regarding relative job worth (e.g., through the use of job evaluation procedures), they adhere to them in setting pay rates.[5]

---

[5] The pertinent part of the decision reads (*County of Washington* v. *Gunther*: 18):

Petitioner argues strenuously that the approach of the Court of Appeals places "the pay structure of virtually every employer and the entire economy . . . at risk and subject to scrutiny by the federal courts." Brief for Petitioners, at 99-100. It raises the spectre that "Title VII plaintiffs could draw any type of comparison imaginable concerning job duties and pay between any job predominantly performed by women and any job predominantly performed by men." *Id.*, at 101. But whatever the merit of petitioner's arguments in other contexts, they are

Recently one district court has directly supported the comparable worth contention—that jobs should be paid in proportion to their relative worth. In April 1981 the U.S. District Court for Western Pennsylvania, in *Martha L. Taylor et al.* v. *Charley Brothers Company and Teamsters Local 30* (78-138), held that the employer, a wholesale grocer, had discriminated against women by assigning them to a separate department from men and paying them substantially less than those in an all-male department doing jobs that were different in their content but similar in their requirements (paragraph 19): "Defendant Charley Brothers intentionally discriminated against . . . women in Department 2 by paying them substantially less than the men in Department 1 because they worked in a department populated only by women, and not because the jobs they performed were inherently worth less than the jobs performed by the men, all in violation of Title VII." A job evaluation undertaken by the plaintiffs provided the basis for the judgment that the pay differences were not due to the fact that the jobs the women performed were inherently worth less.

Although the major legislation on employment discrimination in the United States has no language explicitly incorporating the principle of equal pay for work of equal value,[6] the concept is widely endorsed abroad. Over 80 member nations of the International Labour Organisation have ratified Convention 100, which encourages each member to "promote . . . and ensure the application to all workers of the principle of equal remuneration for men and women workers for work of equal value." Great Britain's 1970 Equal Employment Opportunity Act provides for equal remuneration for men and women employed in "like work" or "work of same or a broadly similar nature" or "work rated as equivalent, having been given an 'equal value' in a job evaluation

---

inapplicable here, for claims based on the type of job comparisons petitioner describes are manifestly different from respondents' claim. Respondents contend that the County of Washington evaluated the worth of their jobs; that the county determined that they should be paid approximately 95% as much as the male correctional officers; that it paid them only about 70% as much, while paying the male officers the full evaluated worth of their jobs; and that the failure of the county to pay respondents the full evaluated worth of their jobs can be proven to be attributable to intentional sex discrimination. Thus, respondents' suit does not require a court to make its own subjective assessment of the value of the male and female guard jobs, or to attempt by statistical technique or other method to quantify the effect of sex discrimination on the wage rates.

[6] It is interesting to note, however, that there is an instance of federal legislation using comparable worth language. The Civil Service Reform Act of 1978, in the section on Merit System Principles (5 USC 2301.(b)(3)), states: "Equal pay should be provided for work of equal value. . . ."

study" (International Labour Office, 1975:12). Canada's Equal Pay and Equal Opportunity Law, which went into effect in spring 1978 for the federal government and publicly chartered industries such as the railroads, airlines, and broadcasting companies, calls for equal pay for work of equal value. Work of equal value is not explicitly defined, but the criteria to be applied in the comparisons are the "composite of skill, effort, and responsibility" as well as working conditions.[7] The Canadian Human Rights Commission, which expects the "composite of skill, effort, and responsibility" to be determined by the use of job evaluation techniques, has established a set of guidelines to assess those job evaluation systems currently in use. Initial efforts at enforcement, however, have not gone beyond cases similar to some of the broader cases brought under the U.S. Equal Pay Act. The Canadian commission has recommended, for example, that female nurses be paid at the same rate as male hospital technicians, a case similar to one in the United States in which female nurse's aides were judged to do work equal to that of male orderlies (Perlman and Ennis, 1980). In Australia, where minimum wages are set for most organizations by state and federal wage boards, the Federal Tribunal adopted a policy of equal pay for work of equal value in 1975. Since that time, the average earnings of full-time female workers have increased substantially relative to those of male workers (Gregory and Duncan, 1981). In all these examples of private and public actions in the United States and abroad, the comparable worth issue raises questions about compensation practices.

## THE ISSUES

In this context the committee interprets the charge from the EEOC to study the validity of compensation systems and methods for determining the relative worth of jobs as requiring an investigation of whether and to what extent existing pay differences between jobs are the result of discrimination.

---

[7] The language of both the American Equal Pay Act and the Canadian Equal Pay and Equal Opportunity Law derives from principles used in job evaluation. Skill, effort, responsibility, and working conditions are the job features most often measured in job evaluation plans. These job features are chosen because they are widely regarded as compensable; that is, these are the aspects of jobs that make them worthy of compensation and that differentiate levels of compensation. In factor point job evaluation plans, compensable features are called factors. Each job is given a numerical rating on each factor, and the scores are added for a total job worth score (Treiman, 1979). Most interpretations of the U.S. law in effect require that two jobs have equal scores on every dimension to be considered equal under the law, whereas the word "composite" in the Canadian law is presumably meant to indicate that jobs can be considered equal if their total scores are equal.

Many people argue that the wages set by the market determine precisely what jobs are worth to both employers and employees, but this position has been explicitly challenged by those who argue that existing wage differences incorporate discriminatory elements. As noted in the committee's interim report (Treiman, 1979), most job evaluation plans, which provide the bases for many employers' compensation programs, use market wage rates to determine the value of features they identify as contributing to job worth (typically, skill, effort, responsibility, and working conditions). That is, how much each feature contributes to the job worth score (the weight of each factor) is determined by studying, with the aid of statistical techniques, how those features appear to be compensated by market wage rates. But if market wage rates incorporate any bias based on sex, race, or ethnicity, then alternative methods for determining job comparability, or ways to remove such bias, are needed. Therefore, our investigation of job comparability required us to examine the bases for wage differentials.

We did not limit the scope of our investigation to particular legal postures, rules, or definitions. As we suggest above, the state of the law regarding comparable worth cases remains in flux. The same can be said for the legal definition of "equal" under the Equal Pay Act and of "discrimination" under Title VII.

The committee and individual members have used various definitions of discrimination to guide and shape our work. Because of this process and because there is no hard-and-fast agreement among committee members—or among legislators or the public—about the precise meaning of discrimination, or about the proper ways of identifying discrimination, we do not offer a single, absolute definition of discrimination. All members of the committee do agree that an essential element of the kind of discrimination we are concerned with here is inequitable treatment based on a person's sex, race, or ethnicity. On that basis we developed working definitions of employment discrimination and wage discrimination.

Employment discrimination exists when one class of people is denied access to higher-paying jobs solely or partly on the basis of social characteristics. If, for example, women or minority men are denied access to managerial positions solely or partly because of their sex or minority status—that is discrimination. This pattern of disparate treatment is not easy to detect and is often difficult to measure or prove, but when provable it is illegal under Title VII of the 1964 Civil Rights Act. As a result of denial of access to better-paying jobs, women and minorities earn lower wages on the average than do men and nonminorities.

Wage discrimination exists when individuals of one social category are paid less than individuals of another social category for reasons that have little or nothing to do with the work they do. There are two major types of wage discrimination:

1. One type of wage discrimination occurs when one class of people is paid less than another class for doing exactly or substantially the same job: for example, male and female machine assemblers (or truck drivers, secretaries, elementary school teachers, professors, etc.) working side by side, doing jobs that are essentially indistinguishable from one another, producing similar results. This kind of wage discrimination is relatively easy to detect and is illegal under the legislation enacted in the early 1960s.

2. A second type of wage discrimination, on which this committee focused intently, arises when the job structure within a firm is substantially segregated by sex, race, or ethnicity, and workers of one category are paid less than workers of another category when the two groups are performing work that is not the same but that is, in some sense, of comparable worth to their employer. The committee grappled with precisely what the phrase "in some sense" involves, and the more technical portions of this report focus at length on how measures of comparable worth might be used. This type of discrimination is difficult to detect, and its legal status is unclear.

Five aspects of our study should be kept in mind by the reader. First, in discussing wage discrimination, particularly of the second type, we say nothing about the question of intent. How pay inequities have come about—through willful exclusion, conscious underpayment, or inadvertent use of practices that have discriminatory effects—is not addressed in our discussion. Our use of the word "discrimination" does not necessarily imply intent.

Second, primarily because we have focused on the second type of wage discrimination, which appears to affect women more than minority men (see Chapter 2), our discussion of sex discrimination is more complete than our discussion of discrimination against minorities. This does not reflect any judgment on our part about the relative importance of sex discrimination and discrimination based on race or ethnicity.

Third, we have not attempted to survey all the methods used to determine rates of pay in the United States. There is a wide variety of compensation systems, ranging from extremely informal to highly formal codified plans, in use today. Each of these plans reflects what employers (and sometimes employees) regard as the compensable features of jobs and helps determine what the jobs are worth to them. Because formal systems of job evaluation make explicit the bases for the comparison of jobs and job worth, our review of compensation practices is limited to formal job evaluation plans.

Fourth, we make no judgments regarding the relative value of jobs to employers or to society or the appropriate relationships among the pay rates for various jobs. The concept of intrinsic job worth—whether it exists, on what it should be based, whether there is a just wage—has been a matter of dispute for many centuries. We do not believe that the value—or worth—of jobs can be determined by scientific methods. Hierarchies of job worth are always, at least in part, a reflection of values.[8] Our concern in this report is limited to assessing whether and to what extent current practices of assessing the worth of jobs and assigning relative pay rates incorporate discriminatory elements. For this purpose we accept the criteria of job worth developed by those who use job evaluation plans and ask such questions as whether the criteria are adequately measured by the features of jobs identified and the measurement techniques used and, in particular, whether elements of discrimination enter the process and, if so, how they can be removed. While many measurement problems are involved in comparing the worth of jobs within an establishment, we do not believe that these problems are insurmountable in principle. They are surmountable, with proper attention to changes in job content and developments in the methodology of job analysis, scaling, and the like.[9]

Fifth, we have confined our discussion to the use of job evaluation plans within individual firms. Because employers use many different job evaluation plans, because the economic circumstances of employers and industries differ, and because we do not believe that there is a hierarchy of job worth that could or should be applied to the entire economy, we look only at the comparable worth approach as it could be used to adjust the pay rates of jobs within individual firms.[10]

---

[8] It is of interest to note, however, that there is a general consistency, although not an exact correspondence, in the relative pay rates of jobs in different societies (Treiman, 1977;108–111), which suggests that some features of jobs are valued quite universally.

[9] The Committee on Occupational Classification and Analysis prepared a report for the Department of Labor on the *Dictionary of Occupational Titles*, addressing many issues concerning the measurement of jobs (see Miller et al., 1980).

[10] This is not to say that we see any difficulty in the application of job evaluation procedures on an industrywide basis, as is currently done in the steel industry. But this is a decision properly left to those in the industry, employers and employees. When compensation is organized on an industrywide basis, job evaluation procedures, as part of the compensation system, would be expected to be similarly organized.

## PLAN OF THE REPORT

We have organized our investigation of the issue of comparable worth in the following way. First, we review the evidence on the extent of wage differentials between men and women and investigate the proximate causes—those variables identified by economists and sociologists as likely to account for some part of the differentials. We then broaden our perspective to consider the institutional context within which wages are determined and workers are allocated to jobs, in order to interpret the findings and to identify features of labor market operations that may account for the unexplained portion of wage differentials. Next we assess various approaches and procedures for formally evaluating the worth of jobs and suggest some procedures that hold promise for identifying and reducing bias where it exists in job worth scores and in wage rates. Finally, we draw together our conclusions from the study.

Chapter 2 documents the substantial difference in earnings between women and men and notes that the difference has not declined over time. We consider what may account for this earnings gap. A selective review of the sociological and economic literature shows that research has accounted for some of the difference in earnings by differences in the characteristics of workers (for example, years of experience and schooling) and in jobs (for example, the requirements of jobs as measured by the *Dictionary of Occupational Titles*) that are generally regarded as legitimate bases for wage differentials. A somewhat different literature points to the pervasiveness of occupational and job segregation by sex, and to the fact that jobs held mainly by women tend to be paid less than jobs held mainly by men. In Chapter 3 we consider the possibility that in some cases wages for some jobs are depressed at least in part *because* the jobs are held mainly by women.

Chapter 3 explores the institutional context within which wages are set and labor is allocated, in order to understand why differences in earnings between men and women persist. In our view, labor markets reflect a complicated set of institutional and other forces that help to explain the persistence of the earnings differential. We attempt to show how such factors as labor market segmentation, job segregation, and employment practices permit the persistence of earnings differentials between men and women. We conclude that there is some basis for believing that intentional and unintentional discriminatory elements enter into the determination of wages and are not likely to disappear, given the current operation of the labor market. And because market wage rates are likely to incorporate the effects of institutional features, which sometimes include discrimination, they may not be unbiased indicators of job worth; hence, some attention to remedies is warranted.

Chapter 4 explores remedies, in particular those based on the use of a job evaluation system to identify and possibly correct bias in the process of setting wages for particular jobs. In enterprises in which job evaluation plans already exist (and hence can be presumed to provide a standard of job worth acceptable to the employer), such plans can be used to identify possible instances of wage discrimination within a firm. A suspicion of discrimination exists if the wages of jobs held mainly by one sex, race, or ethnic group do not correspond on the average to their job worth scores. In the committee's interim report, three characteristics of job evaluation systems that make their use problematic in this context were identified. First, job evaluation is an inherently subjective method, in which well-known processes of sex stereotyping may be operating, resulting in undervaluation of jobs held mainly by women. Second, job worth scores are highly dependent on the choice of compensable features and the weights assigned to them; since most job evaluation plans use market wage rates to establish factor weights, the weights will incorporate the effects of any discrimination that exists in market wages. Third, many employers use different plans for different sectors of their firms (for example, one plan for plant jobs and another for office jobs), so the worth of jobs cannot be compared across all the jobs in those firms. In addition to these inadequacies, we note in Chapter 4 that there are a number of statistical inadequacies in job evaluation procedures as they are currently practiced. We conclude that these features of job evaluation plans make it impossible at the present time to recommend without reservation the use of job evaluation procedures to establish the relative worth of jobs for the resolution of disputes over pay discrimination. Nevertheless, the committee believes that when a job evaluation plan is used as the basis for establishing pay rates within a firm, it can aid in identifying potential wage discrimination. Although job evaluation plans are not perfect metrics, they are of some use. Moreover, we suggest improvements that can be made in job evaluation plans to improve their usefulness; in particular, we suggest procedures to reduce the bias inherent in weights that are based on market wages. These procedures are still in an experimental stage, however, and the committee concludes that there is not sufficient scientific basis to support their imposition on employers by regulatory agencies at the present time.

Chapter 5 summarizes the conclusions that we draw from our investigation of methods for determining the comparable worth of jobs.

# 2 Evidence Regarding Wage Differentials

## THE EXISTENCE OF WAGE DIFFERENTIALS

In the United States today, women earn less than men on the average and minorities earn less than nonminorities on the average. In 1978 women of all races who worked full time all year earned 55 percent as much as white men, and black men earned 72 percent as much as white men (Table 1). Moreover, although schooling has been consistently found to be closely correlated with earnings, at every level of schooling women and black men have lower earnings than white men (Table 2). For example, black men with some college education have lower mean earnings than white men who are high school graduates and only slightly higher mean earnings than white men who have not graduated from high school; and both black and white women who are college graduates have lower mean earnings than white men with eighth-grade educations.[1]

The difference in income between white men and "black and other" men who work full time all year has tended to decline over the past two decades (see Table 3). Between 1955 and 1975, for example, about 40 percent of the difference was eliminated. We do note, however, that

---

[1] These data are based on reports of what people with these characteristics say they actually earn. Full-time year-round work is defined as 35 or more hours per week, 50 or more weeks per year. It is possible that within this category, if the amount of time actually worked by men and women were taken into account, the earnings ratio presented in Table 2 would be slightly different (see note 8).

*13*

TABLE 1   Mean Earnings of Year-Round Full-Time Civilian
Workers 18 Years Old and Over, 1978

|  | Men | Women | Percentage of Earnings of White Men | |
|---|---|---|---|---|
|  |  |  | Men | Women |
| All races | $17,547 | $9,939 | 97.7 | 55.3 |
| White | 17,959 | 9,992 | 100.0 | 55.6 |
| Black | 12,898 | 9,388 | 71.8 | 52.3 |
| Spanish origin[a] | 13,002 | 8,654 | 72.4 | 48.2 |

[a] Persons of Spanish origin may be of any race.

SOURCE: U.S. Bureau of the Census, 1980:Table 57.

the gap between minority family income and nonminority family income, after a period of decline during the 1960s, has remained constant or increased. These divergent trends reflect the effects of many underlying factors, of which the most important are the growing unemployment and declining labor force participation of minority men and the growing proportion among minority families of single-parent families headed by women. They highlight the dangers, especially for minorities, of assessing general progress by referring only to full-time year-round workers.[2]

By contrast, the difference in income between women and white men who work full time all year has failed to show any decline (see Table 3). The aggregate pattern is a combination of the somewhat dissimilar experiences of white women and black and other women. During the late 1950s and early 1960s the income disparity between white women and white men was growing, and over the last 20 years this disparity has remained essentially unchanged. Over the same period much of the racial component of the difference in income between black and other women and white men was eliminated, a fact that has reduced the overall gap but left these women in approximately the same position as white women. Since the mid-1970s, when black and other women achieved virtual parity with white women, the income disparity vis-a-vis white men has not declined further.

Charged with assessing methods for determining job comparability, our focus is properly on the earnings inequalities among workers who

[2] There is a substantial literature on differences in earnings by race, which discusses the measurement of trends and suggests that the process resulting in race differentials is somewhat different from that resulting in sex differentials (see, for example, Freeman, 1973; Welch, 1973; Smith and Welch, 1977; and Reich, 1981).

TABLE 2  Mean Annual Earnings of Year-Round Full-Time Workers by Education, Race, and Sex, 1978

| Years of Education | Mean Earnings | | | | Percentage of Earnings of White Men | | |
|---|---|---|---|---|---|---|---|
| | White Men | Black Men | White Women | Black Women | Black Men | White Women | Black Women |
| Elementary | | | | | | | |
| less than 8 years | $11,303 | $ 9,305 | $ 6,757 | $ 6,388 | 82.3 | 59.8 | 56.5 |
| 8 years | 13,322 | 9,893 | 7,642 | 6,706 | 74.3 | 57.4 | 50.3 |
| High school | | | | | | | |
| 1 to 3 years | 14,183 | 11,221 | 8,124 | 7,413 | 79.1 | 57.3 | 52.3 |
| 4 years | 16,026 | 12,813 | 9,293 | 9,138 | 80.0 | 58.0 | 57.0 |
| College | | | | | | | |
| 1 to 3 years | 17,626 | 14,611 | 10,295 | 10,392 | 82.9 | 58.4 | 59.0 |
| 4 years | 22,975 | 18,242 | 11,866 | 12,539 | 79.4 | 51.6 | 54.6 |
| 5 years or more | 27,476 | 19,945 | 15,607 | 13,538 | 72.6 | 56.8 | 49.3 |
| TOTAL | 17,959 | 12,898 | 9,992 | 9,388 | 71.8 | 55.6 | 52.3 |

SOURCE: U.S. Bureau of the Census, 1980:Table 51.

TABLE 3   Median Income of Year-Round Full-Time Workers by
Sex and Race, 1955–1978[a]

| Year | Median Income of White Men | Percentage of Income of White Men | | | | |
| | | White Women | Black and Other Women | Black Women | Black and Other Men | Black Men |
| --- | --- | --- | --- | --- | --- | --- |
| 1955–1959 | $ 4,874 | 63.2 | 36.4 | n.a.[b] | 60.6 | n.a.[b] |
| 1960–1964 | 6,017 | 59.5 | 38.8 | n.a.[b] | 63.9 | n.a.[b] |
| 1965–1969 | 7,697 | 57.8 | 42.8 | n.a.[b] | 65.8 | n.a.[b] |
| 1970–1974 | 10,893 | 57.1 | 50.4 | 49.3 | 70.7 | 68.3 |
| 1975–1978 | 14,811 | 58.6 | 55.8 | 55.0 | 75.3 | 72.9 |

[a] Table refers to income since earnings data are not available; income data are not available separately for blacks prior to 1967.
[b] Not available.

SOURCE: Computed from U.S. Bureau of the Census, Current Population Reports, Series P-60, Numbers 60, 66, 75, 80, 85, 90, 97, 99, 107, 116, 120, 123, 125.

actually hold jobs. We have further chosen to concentrate primarily on analyzing inequalities between male job-holders and female job-holders, for three reasons. First, as we note above, for full-time year-round workers the difference in earnings between men and women is greater than that between minorities and nonminorities, and the difference in earnings between men and women has not declined while the difference in earnings between minorities and nonminorities has declined. Second, as we note below, the extent of occupational segregation—the degree to which different groups hold different rather than similar jobs—is greater by sex than by race, and this segregation is the very situation that evokes an interest in methods for determining the comparable worth of dissimilar jobs. Third, most of the available research on comparable worth considers sex differentials. Nonetheless, despite the apparently greater immediate relevance of the comparable worth issue to women than to minorities, our analysis is applicable whenever substantial job segregation between different groups exists and whenever particular jobs are dominated by particular groups.

How can one account for the difference in earnings between men and women? Two kinds of explanations have been proposed: those that focus on the characteristics of workers and those that focus on the characteristics of jobs. Of the first kind are studies that attempt to relate pay differences between the races and the sexes to differences that are believed to affect productivity, such as training and experience. Of the second kind are studies that explicitly recognize that earnings differ among jobs and focus on the substantial segregation of the labor force into different jobs on the basis of sex and race as a major explanation of the differences in earnings.

This chapter reviews evidence regarding the sources of earnings differentials between men and women with only occasional reference, for the reasons given above, to racial and ethnic earnings differentials. We begin with studies that focus on the characteristics of workers, then consider those that focus on the characteristics of jobs, reviewing the principal findings of the relevant bodies of research. Because of the vast literature involved, our survey is selective rather than comprehensive.

## THE EFFECT OF WORKER CHARACTERISTICS ON DIFFERENCES IN EARNINGS

In recent years a substantial amount of research has been done by economists and sociologists attempting to explain differences in earnings between men and women on the basis of differences in their personal characteristics. Most of this research has been based implicitly or explicitly on a "human capital" approach. The human capital approach derives from the neoclassical economic theory of wages, which treats wages, the price of labor, like all other prices and posits that, in the absence of discrimination, equilibrium wages will be just equal to the marginal revenue product of labor. In noneconomic terms this means that in the absence of discrimination workers will be paid an amount exactly equal to the value of their economic contribution to a firm. Hence, according to human capital theory, it should be possible in principle to measure directly the extent of inequalities in earnings due to discrimination by comparing wage differences between men and women with differences in their economic contribution, or "productivity"; wage differences not accounted for by differences in productivity could then presumably be ascribed to discrimination.

There are a number of difficulties in such calculations. One difficulty is that wages may not reflect the entire reward paid for a job. Another, more difficult problem is that, with the exception of a few jobs involving the production of physical goods (e.g., coal mining, button sewing), for which the amount produced is easily measured (and for which workers are often paid on a piecework basis), differences in productivity among jobs are virtually impossible to measure. When attempts have been made to measure productivity directly (see, for example, Malkiel and Malkiel, 1973), the researchers themselves usually acknowledge the unsatisfactory nature of the exercise. To get around this problem, researchers using the human capital approach have attempted to estimate productivity indirectly by assuming that differences in productivity among workers derive from differences in their stock of "human capital," that is, their education and training, work experience, continuity of work history, effort or commitment, health, etc., all of which can be measured more or less directly (Schultz, 1961; Mincer, 1970; Becker, 1975).[3]

The basic procedure in human capital studies of earnings differences between men and women is to estimate what their average earnings would be if men and women received an equal return on their human capital and the only differences in their earnings were those due to differences in the amount of their human capital, which are considered to be proxies for differences in productivity. Such estimates are then used to decompose the total difference in average earnings into that part due to differences in human capital—and, presumably, productivity—and that part due to differences in the rate of return on investments in human capital—often assumed to represent discrimination. (A more detailed discussion of these procedures is presented in the technical note at the end of this chapter.)

Some problematic features of this approach should be noted before reviewing the evidence based on it. First, the marginal productivity theory of wages is not universally accepted. Many argue that factors other than productivity, such as custom, union strength, and the economic viability of an industry or enterprise, affect wages (e.g., Bibb and Form, 1977; Phelps-Brown, 1977; Piore, 1979). Second, human capital variables are of unknown quality as proxies for productivity differences. "Experience," for example, may reflect either productivity-enhancing, on-the-job learning or simply seniority: in observing a correlation between wages and experience, one does not know to what extent it is higher productivity or greater seniority that is associated with higher pay.[4] Third, the link between concepts and indicators is often quite

---

[3] Various indicators of labor force commitment are often included in earnings equations because the degree of commitment could affect the quality of work effort and hence productivity. For example, it is sometimes argued that marriage reduces the productivity of women but increases that of men because married women adjust their work lives to accommodate their family obligations, while married men are motivated by their family responsibilities to increase their earning power; marital status is therefore often included as an explanatory variable.

[4] The idea that wages rise with experience because workers are making on-the-job investments in productivity-enhancing human capital is not universally accepted. Some (e.g., Edwards, 1977) argue that experience should be interpreted as a proxy for seniority rather than for productivity: that is, wages rise with experience as a result of seniority or tenure provisions that reflect normative expectations that older workers or long-time employees should earn more regardless of their level of productivity.

tenuous. For example, even those who accept the idea that education enhances productivity do not necessarily accept "years of school completed" as a good indicator of the quality and extent of job-specific skills learned in school. Finally, to interpret as discrimination all earnings differences between groups that are not accounted for by the variables explicitly studied (that is, the "residual difference") requires two very strong assumptions. The first assumption is that all relevant factors are measured: "all relevant factors" includes all factors that underlie differences in productivity and that are distinct from all other factors.[5] The second assumption is that all factors are measured without error.[6] In practice, however, these assumptions are virtually never completely satisfied; at best, there is no way of being certain to what extent they are satisfied. Hence, there is always a degree of doubt as to the validity of the empirical findings regarding discrimination.

Let us now turn to the empirical literature.[7] Table 4 summarizes the findings from several studies—based on data from national samples of the working population—that attempt to account for differences in earnings between men and women on the basis of the characteristics of workers. In most of the studies, worker characteristics account for very little of the difference in earnings; in fact, only two of the studies can explain more than one-fifth of the difference between men's and women's average earnings in terms of differences in worker characteristics. The two studies whose findings go furthest toward explaining the observed earnings gap, those by Mincer and Polachek (1974) and by Corcoran and Duncan (1979), account for less than half the difference. The relative success of these two studies in explaining the earnings difference can be attributed largely to their use of a measure of actual labor market experience that is more complete than those usually available.

The study by Corcoran and Duncan (1979) is perhaps the most thor-

[5] This assumption invites consideration in each specific case of what additional factors might create differences in productivity between women and men and thereby reduce the unexplained part of the difference in earnings. It must be understood, however, that in order for such additional factors to contribute to an explanation of the difference, they must be correlated with sex, correlated with earnings, and relatively uncorrelated with factors already in the equation; otherwise they will add little or nothing to the explanation of the difference in earnings that results from this type of statistical analysis. (Of course, omitting variables that are correlated with variables included in the prediction equation biases the coefficients of the included variables but does not particularly affect the predictions, which are the focus of interest here.)

[6] The term "measurement error" here encompasses issues of reliability, validity, functional form, and error structure—all of which can create seriously misleading results with the regression procedures that are usually used in these studies.

[7] Many of these studies have been summarized previously by Kohen (1975).

TABLE 4  Summary of Studies Accounting for Sex Differences in Earnings on the Basis of Worker Characteristics Only

| Author | Data Source and Population Studied | Measure of Earnings | Statistical Method and Explanatory Variables[a] | Women's Earnings as a Percentage of Men's[b] | | Percentage of Gap Explained[d] |
|---|---|---|---|---|---|---|
| | | | | Observed | Adjusted[c] | |
| *Representative national samples* | | | | | | |
| Blinder | SID:[e] White employed household heads, age 25+, and employed spouses | 1969 mean hourly earnings | R, S: 2, 9, 11, 12, 13, 14 | 56 | 56 | 0 |
| Corcoran and Duncan | SID:[e] White employed household heads and employed spouses, age 18–64 | 1975 hourly earnings | R, S: 1, 5, 6, 9, 11, 12, 13, 14, 17 | 74 | 85 | 44 |
| Gwartney and Stroup | Census: U.S. population, age 25+ | Med. annual inc. 1959 | F, R: 1, 2 | 33 | 39 | 9 |
| | | Med. annual inc. 1969 | F, R: 1, 2 | 32 | 40 | 12 |
| | Full-time, year-round workers | Mean annual inc. 1959 | F, R: 1, 2 | 56 | 58 | 4 |
| Oaxaca[f] | SEO: Urban employees, age 16+  White | 1967 hourly earnings | R, S: 1, 3, 7–10, 12, 13 | 65 | 72 | 20 |
| | Black | | | 67 | 69 | 6 |
| Sawhill | CPS:[h] Wage and salary workers | 1966 annual earnings | R:  1, 3, 10, 13 | 46 | 56 | 18 |
| *National samples, restricted age* | | | | | | |
| Kohen and Roderick | NLS:[i] Nonstudent, full-time wage and salary workers, age 18–25  White | 1968–1969 hourly earnings | R, S: 1, 3, 4, 7–9, 13–15 | 76 | 78 | 8 |
| | Black | | | 82 | 81 | −6 |
| Mincer and Polachek | NLS;[i] SEO:[g] Married white wage and salary workers, age 30–44 | 1967 hourly earnings | R, S: 1, 6, 11 | 66 | 80 | 41 |

[a] Statistical methods: F = frequency distribution or tabular standardization, R = regression analysis, S = separate equations for males and females.

Explanatory variables:

1. Education
2. Age
3. Race
4. Mental ability (intelligence)
5. Formal training
6. Actual labor market experience
7. Proxy for labor market experience
8. Marital status
9. Health
10. Hours of work (annual, weekly, full-time/part-time)
11. Tenure (length of service with current employer)
12. Size of city of residence
13. Region of residence
14. Socioeconomic backgound (parental education, occupation, income, number of siblings, migration history, ethnicity, etc.)
15. Quality of schooling
16. Record of absenteeism
17. Dual burden (number of children, limits on hours or location, plans to stop work for reasons other than training, etc.)

[b] Average female earnings expressed as a percentage of average male earnings.

[c] Adjusted earnings indicate the ratio of female to male earnings if the two sexes had the same average levels (or composition) on the explanatory variables. When several adjustments are presented in the original study their average is shown here.

[d] This is given by (expected − observed)/(100 − observed).

[e] SID = Panel Study of Income Dynamics

[f] Oaxaca also conducted some investigations using job characteristics as well as worker characteristics (see Table 10).

[g] SEO = Survey of Economic Opportunity

[h] CPS = Current Population Survey

[i] NLS = National Longitudinal Surveys (Parnes)

ough of this genre of studies, including detailed measures of educational attainment, work history, on-the-job training, and attachment to the labor force for a national sample of household heads and their spouses who were in the labor force in 1975.[8] This study explicitly excluded occupation as an explanatory variable in order to provide a pure test of the human capital approach. According to human capital theory, individuals invest in human capital as long as they expect future returns to compensate them for foregone earnings and other costs of acquiring human capital. With perfect opportunity for mobility and perfect availability of information, people should seek the highest return for their human capital in the labor market; thus, over the long run, market competition should equalize the returns on human capital across occupations and industries. Differences in returns on human capital for those employed in different occupations must then, according to the theory, be taken as reflecting past or present market imperfections, including institutional barriers and discriminatory practices.

Table 5 shows Corcoran and Duncan's decomposition of the difference in earnings between white men and white women. According to their formulation, a little less than half (44 percent) of the difference in the mean earnings of men and women can be attributed to differences in education, work experience, and labor force attachment, and virtually all of this is due to differences in work history—women have less overall work experience, less previous experience with the current employer, and less on-the-job training. Interestingly, indicators of labor force attachment account for almost none of the gap, a finding that suggests to Corcoran and Duncan that although women may stay out of the labor force because of family obligations, losing valuable years of experience, when they do work their "dual obligation" (to the family as well as to the job) does not negatively affect their earnings potential (see also Corcoran, 1979).

Exactly how experience affects earnings and whether experience has the same consequences for men and for women are questions currently subject to considerable debate (see, e.g., Mincer and Polachek, 1974; Edwards, 1977; also see below). We have already noted alternative interpretations of the relationship between experience, productivity, and

[8] In Corcoran and Duncan's sample, the hourly wages of women averaged about 75 percent of those of men, a figure somewhat higher than the often-cited 60 percent ratio in annual earnings of full-time year-round workers. It is unclear what accounts for this disparity, although one possibility is that Corcoran and Duncan's data are controlled for the number of hours that "full-time" workers actually work. Women may work fewer hours than men, a possibility that, if not controlled, would exaggerate the size of the difference in their earnings. Another possibility is that differences in the nature of the samples (the Corcoran and Duncan data are from a sample of families rather than individuals) create differences in the earnings ratios.

TABLE 5   Decomposition of the Wage Differential Between
Employed White Men and White Women

| Explanatory Variables | Percentage of 1975 Hourly Wage Gap Explained | |
|---|---|---|
| Work History | 39 | |
| Years out of labor force since completing school | | 6 [a] |
| Years of work experience before current employer (plus square) | | 3 |
| Years with current employer prior to current position | | 12 |
| Years of training completed on current job | | 11 |
| Years of post-training tenure on current job | | −1 |
| Proportion of total working years that were full time | | 8 |
| Indications of labor force attachment | 3 | |
| Hours of work missed due to illness | | 0 |
| Hours of work missed due to illness of others | | −1 |
| Placed limits on job hours or location | | 2 |
| Plans to stop work for reasons other than training | | 2 |
| Formal education (years of school completed) | 2 | |
| PERCENTAGE EXPLAINED | 44 | |
| PERCENTAGE UNEXPLAINED | 56 | |
| TOTAL | 100 | |

[a] These percentages are derived by Corcoran and Duncan for each variable by the formula

$$c_i = (\Delta Z_i - \hat{\beta}_{iwm})/(\ln W_{wm} - \ln W_{wf}),$$

where $\Delta Z_i$ is the difference in means between white men and white women on variable $i$, $\hat{\beta}_{iwm}$ is the regression coefficient of variable $i$ for white men, $\ln W_{wm}$ is the natural log of mean hourly wages for white men, and $\ln W_{wf}$ is the same for white women.

SOURCE: Adapted from Corcoran and Duncan, 1979.

earnings. Here we add the observation that returns on experience are generally lower for women than they are for men, which accounts for part of the earnings differential; that is, the earnings differential is not due simply to the lesser experience of women. But the lesser experience of women does need to be explained. The conventional interpretation is that women voluntarily limit their labor force experience because of the demands of their family responsibilities. Some, however, would argue that the difference in labor force experience between men and women, particularly in the kind of experience that may be most relevant to earnings (on-the-job training), may itself reflect discriminatory restriction of occupational opportunities. For example, employers may be reluctant to hire or to train women because they assume that women will leave the labor force to bear or raise children (Sawhill, 1973). Or the difference in the amount of on-the-job training between women and men may be largely the result of institutional practices that tend to exclude women (Duncan and Hoffman, 1978). To the extent that differences between men and women in the characteristics thought to affect income themselves result from discriminatory processes in employment and training, empirical estimates of the extent of discrimination will be too low. This downward bias may somewhat offset the tendency of such estimates to be too high due to the possible omission of additional legitimate determinants of earnings from estimation equations.

In these studies, researchers have consistently found that a substantial part of the earnings difference cannot be explained by factors thought to measure productivity differences. Taken at face value, these results create a presumption of additional factors at work, possibly including institutional barriers and discrimination. Nonetheless, because of the many difficulties inherent in the human capital approach (discussed above), because the consistency of results from these studies may reflect identical flaws in the research, and because the findings concerning discrimination are so indirect (other factors failing to explain fully the difference in earnings rather than discrimination being shown to explain directly the remaining difference), the committee concludes that these studies are suggestive rather than definitive.

## THE EFFECT OF JOB CHARACTERISTICS ON DIFFERENCES IN EARNINGS

It is not surprising that explanations focusing on the characteristics of individual workers leave a substantial portion of the earnings gap unexplained, since occupational differences in earnings are very large and the labor force is substantially segregated by race and by sex. A second category of studies that attempts to explain the earnings differentials between men and women focuses on the characteristics of the jobs they hold. The central fact is that men and women tend to hold different types of jobs. We should note here that we often refer to job segregation rather than occupational segregation. As we argue below, even within finely defined occupations (e.g., lawyer, sales clerk, hairdresser), jobs are frequently segregated by sex. Unfortunately, available data frequently permit comparisons only between occupations, but this empirical limitation should not be allowed to obscure the conceptual distinctions.[9]

---

[9] Jobs are specific positions within establishments or the economic activities of specific individuals. They entail particular duties and responsibilities and involve the performance of particular tasks in particular settings. Examples of jobs include "headwaiter at Lion D'Or in Washington, D.C.," "welder on Assembly Line 3 at the Ford Motors assembly

Table 6 shows the distribution of workers across broad occupational categories by sex and by race. Women are substantially more likely than men to work in clerical and service occupations and less likely than men to work in craft and laboring occupations. Black and other men and all women are less likely to hold managerial jobs than are white men. Black and other men, who are more likely to work in blue-collar occupations than are white men, are less likely to work as craft workers and more likely to hold jobs in the operative and laborer categories. Blacks and others of both sexes, especially women, are more likely to work in service occupations than are whites.

Segregation indices calculated for the distributions across these broad occupational groups provide one way of measuring the extent of occupational segregation. An index of segregation between two groups can be interpreted as the minimum proportion of one group that would have to be shifted for its occupational distribution to be identical to that of the other.[10] For example, in 1970, 44 percent of white women would have had to shift their occupational category for the distribution of white women across broad occupational groups to be identical to that of white men. Occupational segregation by sex has barely decreased at all among whites over the past several decades; it has decreased substantially among minorities, but it still remains high. Table 7 presents these indices as calculated by Treiman and Terrell (1975b:167). The large change in

---

plant in Los Angeles," "seller of leather goods at a street stall on Fifth Avenue in New York," and "cardiologist in private practice in St. Louis." Occupations are aggregations of jobs, grouped on the basis of their similarity in content—that is, similarity in the tasks, duties, and responsibilities they entail and the conditions under which they are performed. Such aggregations may be more or less gross, depending on their purpose.

[10] The segregation index, or index of dissimilarity, $\Delta$, is given as

$$\Delta = \sum \frac{|x_i - y_i|}{2},$$

where $x_i$ is the percentage of one population (e.g., men) in the $i$th category of a classification, and $y_i$ is the percentage of the other population (e.g., women) in the $i$th category (Duncan and Duncan, 1955). $\Delta$ is then the percentage of either population that would have to shift categories to make its distribution exactly equal to that of the other population. Obviously, we would never expect one group to shift completely and the other group not at all (e.g., for women to shift occupations to achieve a distribution exactly like the current distribution of men), since this would result in a major shift in the distribution of the total population over all categories (in this case, a shift in the distribution of the total labor force over occupational groups). It is more plausible to imagine the kinds of shifts that would be required by both groups to create identical distributions without changing the distribution of the total. It can be shown, however, that the sum of the proportions in the two groups required to shift categories to achieve identical distributions in this latter instance is exactly equal to $\Delta$. Hence $\Delta$ is an appropriate measure of the dissimilarity, or segregation, of the two groups.

TABLE 6   Occupational Distribution Over Major Occupational Groups by Race and Sex, 1979

| | White Men | Black and Other Men | White Women | Black and Other Women | Percent Female | Percent Black and Other |
|---|---|---|---|---|---|---|
| White-collar workers | 42.8% | 27.4% | 66.5% | 49.7% | 52.8% | 8.4% |
| Professional and technical | 15.6 | 10.5 | 16.4 | 14.2 | 43.3 | 9.0 |
| Managers and administrators, except farm | 14.9 | 6.9 | 6.8 | 3.4 | 24.5 | 5.5 |
| Sales workers | 6.4 | 2.5 | 7.4 | 3.1 | 45.0 | 4.9 |
| Clerical workers | 6.0 | 7.6 | 35.9 | 29.0 | 80.3 | 10.9 |
| Blue-collar workers | 45.5 | 53.2 | 14.1 | 18.0 | 18.4 | 12.5 |
| Craft and kindred workers | 22.0 | 16.6 | 1.9 | 1.2 | 5.7 | 7.9 |
| Operatives, except transport | 11.2 | 15.4 | 10.2 | 14.7 | 39.9 | 15.1 |
| Transport equipment operatives | 5.6 | 8.5 | .8 | .6 | 8.6 | 14.3 |
| Non-farm laborers | 6.7 | 12.7 | 1.3 | 1.6 | 11.6 | 17.5 |
| Service workers | 7.7 | 15.9 | 18.1 | 31.5 | 62.4 | 19.8 |
| Private household workers | — | .1 | 2.0 | 6.8 | 99.4 | 33.5 |
| Other service workers | 7.7 | 15.7 | 16.1 | 24.6 | 59.1 | 18.5 |
| Farm workers | 4.0 | 3.5 | 1.3 | .8 | 18.3 | 8.9 |
| Farmers and farm managers | 2.5 | .6 | .4 | .1 | 10.1 | 2.8 |
| Farm laborers and supervisors | 1.5 | 2.9 | .9 | .7 | 27.6 | 15.9 |
| TOTAL | 100.0 | 100.0 | 100.0 | 100.0 | 100.0 | 11.3 |
| N (thousands) | (50,721) | (5,779) | (35,304) | (5,141) | 41.7 | — |

SOURCE: U.S. Department of Labor, Bureau of Labor Statistics, 1980b:Table 22.

TABLE 7   Occupational Segregation Indices, 1940–1970

|  | 1940 | 1950 | 1960 | 1970 |
|---|---|---|---|---|
| Occupational segregation by sex among: | | | | |
| Whites | 0.46 | 0.43 | 0.44 | 0.44 |
| Blacks and others | 0.58 | 0.50 | 0.52 | 0.49 |
| Occupational segregation by race among: | | | | |
| Men | 0.43 | 0.36 | 0.35 | 0.30 |
| Women | 0.62 | 0.52 | 0.45 | 0.30 |

Note: Indices are calculated for occupational distributions across 11 major census categories. The data from 1940 to 1960 are classified according to the 1940 census detailed occupational classification; the 1970 data are classified according to the 1960 census detailed occupational classification.

SOURCE: Treiman and Terrell, 1975b:167. Copyright© 1975 by Russell Sage Foundation. Reprinted by permission of the publisher, Russell Sage Foundation.

the occupational distribution of black and other women occurred as they were able to enter clerical and sales jobs and service jobs other than in private households. In 1940, 75 percent of all employed black and other women worked as domestic servants or farm laborers (Treiman and Terrell, 1975b:160); by 1979 only 7 percent worked in domestic service (Table 6).

Since broad occupational groups are made up by aggregating smaller detailed occupations, each of which may be dominated by a particular group, segregation indices that are calculated using detailed occupations are usually larger than those based on broad occupational categories (logically they cannot be smaller). Within the clerical category, for example, mail carriers are mainly (92 percent) men while stenographers are mainly (93 percent) women. Similarly, among craft workers, construction trade workers are virtually entirely (98 percent) men, while a majority of bookbinders, decorators, and window dressers are women (U.S. Bureau of the Census, 1973: Table 1). The U.S. Commission on Civil Rights has calculated segregation indices across approximately 400 detailed census occupational categories. In 1976, the index of occupational segregation between white men and white women was 66.1 and between black women and white men was 69.3 (U.S. Commission on Civil Rights, 1978:42).

Occupational segregation by race is also substantial, although it has declined considerably since 1940. Treiman and Terrell's calculation (see Table 7), based on broad occupational categories, shows that for 1970 the index of occupational segregation by race for both men and women stood at 30. The more detailed categorization used by the U.S. Commission on Civil Rights (for 1976) resulted in an index of occupational segregation between black and white men of 37.9 and between black and white women of 35.8. Regardless of the level of aggregation, occupational segregation is more pronounced by sex than by race. There are 553 occupations with wage and salary earners included in the most disaggregated level of the 1970 U.S. census classification (U.S. Bureau of the Census, 1973:Table 24): 310 of them (more than half) have at least 80 percent male incumbents, and another 50 (9 percent) have at least 80 percent female incumbents. Moreover, 70 percent of the men and 54 percent of the women in the labor force are concentrated in occupations dominated by their own sex.[11]

Not only do women do different work than men, but also the work women do is paid less, and the more an occupation is dominated by women the less it pays (Sommers, 1974). For the 499 wage and salary occupations included in the 1970 census expanded occupational classification (with values on all relevant variables), the solid line in Figure 1 shows the relationship between the percentage female and the median wage and salary earnings for job incumbents of both sexes.[12] For these data, each additional percent female in an occupation results in an average of about $42 less in annual income: overall, "women's work" pays about $4,000 less per year on the average than "men's work."[13]

[11] It is interesting to note that occupations filled mainly (80 percent or more) by men average many fewer incumbents than occupations filled mainly (80 percent or more) by women: 100,363 and 312,144, respectively, in 1970. This difference is sometimes taken to indicate the crowding of women into relatively few occupations; it is probably also a reflection of the propensity of designers of occupational classifications (including the census classification) to make finer distinctions among the occupations filled mainly by men than among those filled mainly by women. For example, although secretarial jobs are probably about as varied as managerial jobs, the census classification includes 36 subgroups within the category "managers and administrators, not elsewhere classified" and only two subgroups within the category "secretaries." Differences in the degree of inclusiveness of occupational categories render somewhat problematic discussions of the degree of occupational segregation. Of course, successive disaggregation of occupational categories can only result in increased (or unchanged) estimates of the degree of segregation.

[12] The earnings figures are adjusted to correct for differences in the estimated number of hours worked per year: annualized median earnings = median annual earnings $\times$ [2,080/ (mean hours worked last week $\times$ median weeks worked last year)]. The constant 2,080 (40 $\times$ 52) is an estimate of the hours of labor contributed by full-time year-round workers.

[13] When average earnings are estimated separately for men and women from the percent female in occupations, the resulting equations are $\hat{Y}_M = 8,324 - 29.6(W)$ and $\hat{Y}_F = 5,761 - 16.3(W)$, respectively, where $W$ is the percent female in each occupation, and $\hat{Y}_M$ and $\hat{Y}_F$ are the estimated annualized wage and salary earnings of men and women. These equations can be interpreted as indicating that on the average each additional percent female of an occupation costs male workers about $30 in annual income and female

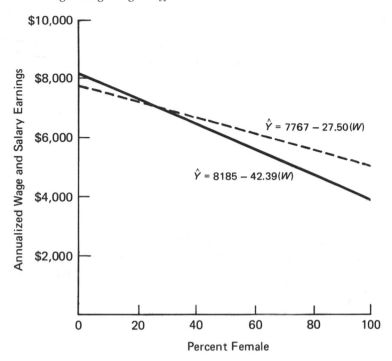

FIGURE 1 Relationship between percent female and annualized median earnings of incumbents for 499 1970 census occupational categories. Solid line is simple regression of mean earnings on percent female. Broken line is regression of mean earnings on percent female controlling for six human capital and job characteristics—see text for details.

workers about $16: men doing "women's work" can expect to earn nearly $3,000 less per year on the average than men doing "men's work"; women doing "men's work" can expect to earn about $1,600 more per year on the average than women doing "women's work."

Because women earn less on the average than men, it is not surprising that occupations dominated by women pay less on the average (the correlation between percent female and mean annualized earnings—the solid line shown in Figure 1—is −.45); nonetheless, it is theoretically possible for the entire difference in average pay to be accounted for by differing distributions of men and women between low-wage and high-wage occupations, with each occupation paying men and women equally. Such a result would indeed be consistent with the finding that the higher the percentage female, the lower the average earnings of both male and female workers. In fact, however, men tend on the average to earn substantially more than women in the same occupation. For occupations with any given male/female ratio, men earn a great deal more on the average than women—the expected difference ranging from more than $1,200 for occupations dominated by women to about $2,400 for occupations dominated by men (or, to express the relation in terms of proportions, women's expected earnings fall from 77 percent to 69 percent of those of men as occupations become increasingly dominated by men).

The relationship between the sex composition of occupations and the earnings of incumbents cannot easily be accounted for on the basis of either the personal characteristics of incumbents or the requirements of the jobs. In a study using the census data described above (Hartmann et al., 1980), the staff attempted to predict the median earnings of incumbents of each occupation from seven variables: mean years of school completed; mean years of postschooling labor force experience;[14] four measures of job requirements derived from data in the *Dictionary of Occupational Titles* (substantive complexity, motor skills, physical demands, and unfavorable working conditions; see Miller et al., 1980, Appendix F); and percent female. The dotted line in Figure 1 shows the relationship between percent female and annualized median earnings, holding constant the other six variables.[15] From the substantial similarity of the solid and dotted lines in the figure it is evident that the differences among occupations with respect to these factors account for relatively little of the relationship between percent female and median earnings (although, of course, they do account for a large portion of the differences among occupations in average earnings).[16] On the basis of these data it appears that the sex composition of occupations, inde-

---

[14] Extent of previous work experience is, unfortunately, not measured directly by the census. For men an adequate proxy can be computed in a straightforward way: mean work experience is estimated by mean age minus mean years of school completed minus 6, on the assumption that on the average men start school when they are 6 and work every year subsequent to completing their schooling. For women, by contrast, such a proxy is inappropriate because large numbers of women leave the labor force after marriage and still larger numbers leave during childbearing years. To achieve a reasonable estimate of the average labor force experience of women in each occupation, an estimation procedure was employed that involves viewing the average labor force experience of women in each occupation as a function of age-specific labor force participation rates and the average age of women in the occupation. See Hartmann et al. (1980) for details on the construction of this measure.

[15] The equation corresponding to this line in the figure was derived by substituting the means of all independent variables except percent female into the equation shown in note 16.

[16] The full equation relating earnings to the other seven characteristics for the 499 census occupations is

$$\hat{Y} = -3341 + 681(E) + 75.2(X) + 217(F_1) + 82.4(F_2)$$
$$- 9.25(F_3) + 23.6(F_4) - 27.5(W),$$

where $Y$ is annualized median earnings of incumbents, $E$ is mean years of school completed by incumbents, $X$ is mean years of labor force experience of incumbents, $F_1$ is the complexity of the occupation, $F_2$ is a measure of the motor skills required by the occupation, $F_3$ is the physical demands required by the occupation, $F_4$ is a measure of undesirable working conditions, and $W$ is the percent female among incumbents. The $R^2$ associated with the equation is .751.

pendent of other occupational characteristics and of average personal characteristics, has a strong effect on the earnings of incumbents.[17]

To assess the role of occupational segregation in accounting for the differences in earnings between men and women, we reviewed a set of studies analogous to the human capital studies reported above but that include the characteristics of the jobs that workers hold as well as the characteristics of workers. Measures of job characteristics include a variety of scales for which scores are available for each category of the census three-digit occupational classification (e.g., prestige; Duncan's socioeconomic index; the median income of male incumbents, an indicator of which occupations are intrinsically high-paying or low-paying; authority exercised on the job; and percent female) as well as classifications of jobs by major industry group, class of worker, major occupational group, and detailed occupational group. Insofar as differences in the sex composition of jobs are associated with differences in pay rates, as they appear to be, the more finely disaggregated an occupational classification is, the larger is the proportion of the total difference in earnings that can be attributed to the segregation of men and women in the labor force.

In studies that adjust only for differences between men and women across large occupational groups, the variables used do not in general account for a large portion of the difference in earnings.[18] For example,

[17] The technical basis for this conclusion is the fact that the net regression coefficient associated with percent female in the equation reported in note 16 is statistically significant ($p \leq .01$). Birnbaum (1979) has argued, however, that simple reliance on a coefficient for gender (or gender composition) to measure discrimination may be misleading since it is possible to generate statistically significant coefficients relating gender and earnings even under a single-factor model in which gender, earnings, and "merit" (legitimate determinants of pay differences) are all determined by an underlying "quality" dimension but are otherwise uncorrelated. This is known as underestimation bias (Madansky, 1959; Cook and Campbell, 1979). He proposes as a test for discrimination that both relations hold: $\beta_{YW \cdot M} < 0$ and $\beta_{MW \cdot Y} > 0$, where $Y$ and $W$ are defined as in note 16, $M$ is a measure of "merit" (in this case the expected earnings predicted by the equation in note 16 with $W$ omitted), and the $\beta$'s are standardized net regression coefficients. Under this criterion discrimination is clearly present, since $\beta_{YW \cdot M} = -.294$ and $\beta_{MW \cdot Y} = .201$; that is, holding constant differences among occupations in the educational attainment and experience of incumbents and in the four occupational characteristics, the higher the percent female the lower the average earnings; and holding constant average earnings, the higher the percent female the higher the overall level of the factors that predict earnings.

[18] One exception is a study by Oaxaca (1973). The job characteristics he used—broad census occupational category, class of worker, industry, and union membership—account for a substantial portion of the difference in earnings. Human capital variables accounted for 20 percent of the male-female difference in earnings among whites and 6 percent among blacks, and the job descriptor variables accounted for an additional 37 percent for whites and 39 percent for blacks. The important variables, however, were industry and union membership; broad occupational group and class of worker explained little of the difference in earnings.

TABLE 8    Annualized Median Earnings[a] by Sex for Census Major
Occupation Groups, 1970

| Census Major Group | Men | Women | Women's Earnings as a Percentage of Men's |
|---|---|---|---|
| Professional, technical, and kindred workers | $9,701 | $7,731 | 79.7 |
| Managers and administrators, except farm | 9,496 | 5,514 | 58.1 |
| Sales workers | 7,684 | 3,185 | 41.4 |
| Clerical and kindred workers | 7,298 | 4,805 | 65.8 |
| Craft and kindred workers | 7,840 | 4,676 | 59.6 |
| Operatives, except transport | 6,544 | 3,936 | 60.1 |
| Transport equipment operatives | 6,351 | 4,064 | 64.0 |
| Laborers, except farm | 5,025 | 3,556 | 70.8 |
| Farmers and farm managers | 4,663 | 2,442 | 52.4 |
| Farm laborers and foremen | 2,364 | 1,495 | 63.2 |
| Service workers, except private household | 5,117 | 3,032 | 59.3 |
| Private household workers | 2,170 | 1,525 | 70.3 |
| TOTAL | 7,394 | 4,603 | 62.3 |
| Average within-category earnings ratio[b] | — | — | 63.4 |

[a] Adjusted to correct for differences in the number of hours worked per year. Annualized median earnings = median earnings × [2080/(mean hours worked last week × median weeks worked last year)]. The constant ( = 40 × 52) is an estimate of the hours of labor contributed by full-time year-round workers.
[b] Weighted average of within-category ratios, with weights equal to total labor force in each category.

SOURCE: U.S. Bureau of the Census, 1973:Table 24.

in a study by Bluestone and his colleagues (1973), education and a classification of occupations into broad census groups accounted for only 6 percent of the difference. Fuchs (1971), using a number of human capital variables and the distinction between private and government wage and salary workers, accounted for 15 percent of the difference. As Table 8 shows, one reason for the lack of explanatory findings is that the differences in earnings within major occupational groups are on average nearly as large as that for the labor force as a whole. The differences in mean earnings within major occupational groups arise in large part from the fact that, within each category, men and women are substantially segregated by specific occupation, the earnings levels of which are often quite different.

Table 9 shows a decomposition of the earnings differences of men and women into a part due to occupational segregation and a part due to within-occupation pay differences for three successively more detailed classifications of 1970 census data. The decomposition is carried out in two ways to cope with the index problem (Oaxaca, 1973); the alternate estimates are shown in column (A) and (B) under each classification. Starting at the left, we note that adjusting for gender differences in distribution over 12 major occupational groups accounts for not more than about 10 percent of the difference in earnings. When 222 categories are used (the middle columns), between 10 and 20 percent of the difference is accounted for by occupational segregation. And when 479 categories are used, occupational segregation accounts for about 35–40 percent of the difference.[19] This exercise illustrates that further analysis of occupational segregation requires much more detailed data than are currently available from the census or from national sample surveys.

Studies that use the job characteristics available for the more detailed occupational classifications in the census and in some national samples (summarized in Table 10) account for more of the difference in earnings between men and women than do those studies using only broad occupational categories. With one exception, these studies account for 30 percent or more of the difference in earnings. The exception, the study by Featherman and Hauser (1976), uses Duncan's socioeconomic index as the occupational descriptor. This index, like prestige scales, in the aggregate gives similar scores to men's and women's jobs and hence would not be expected to account for much of the difference in earnings between men and women.[20] Sanborn (1964) accounts for 71 percent of the difference in earnings, primarily because he uses a detailed occupational classification: it is the different distribution of men and women

---

[19] The portion of the earnings difference between men and women due to earnings differences within occupations would be expected to continue to decrease as the occupational classification used became finer. It would be ideal to have data on the segregation of the labor force into jobs ("job" meaning a collection of positions within a firm involving similar tasks and requiring similar skills; see note 9).

[20] Although the use of prestige scales or Duncan's socioeconomic index does not usually account for much of the difference in earnings between men and women, both the Suter and Miller (1973) and the Treiman and Terrell (1975a) studies, which use these occupational characteristics, account for about two-fifths of the difference. This is almost certainly due to their use of a variable representing actual labor market experience, a variable that generally accounts for a sizable portion of the difference in earnings between men and women because they tend to have significantly different amounts of employment experience (see the discussion of the findings of Corcoran and Duncan, pp. 19–22).

TABLE 9  Decomposition of Earnings Differentials Between Men and Women into Within-Occupation and Between-Occupation Components, for Successively More Detailed Occupational Classifications (1970 Census Data)

| | Census Major Group Classification (N = 12) | | Intermediate Classification (N = 222)[a] | | Census Expanded Occupational Classification (N = 479)[b] | |
|---|---|---|---|---|---|---|
| *Female Earnings as a Percentage of Male Earnings* [c] | | | | | | |
| (1) Male average earnings (annualized)[d] | 100 | | 100 | | 100 | |
| (2) Average earnings of women if they had same income as men in each occupation[e] | 96 | | 93 | | 85 | |
| (3) Average earnings of men if they had same income as women in each occupation[f] | 63 | | 68 | | 76 | |
| (4) Female average earnings[d] | 62 | | 64 | | 63 | |
| *Decomposition of Earnings Differentials*[g] | | | | | | |
| | (A) | (B) | (A) | (B) | (A) | (B) |

| | | | | | | |
|---|---|---|---|---|---|---|
| Due to occupational segregation | 3 | 11 | 11 | 19 | 35 | 41 |
| Due to within-occupation pay differences | 97 | 89 | 89 | 81 | 65 | 59 |
| TOTAL | 100 | 100 | 100 | 100 | 100 | 100 |

[a] Aggregation of the 1970 census detailed occupational classification to a minimum of 1,000 men and 1,000 women in each occupational group (see Treiman, 1973, for details).

[b] The classification used in detailed occupational tabulations published in U.S. Bureau of the Census (1973). Formed by disaggregating selected occupations by industry and class of worker. Only data for occupations with wage and salary earnings reported are used here.

[c] Earnings are annual wage and salary earnings adjusted to account for estimated hours worked per year. Annualized earnings = annual earnings × (2,080/[hours worked last week × weeks worked last year]) since 2,080 = 40 × 53 = full-time year-round work. Data for each occupational category are either the mean or the median. The use of the median rather than the mean introduces some error into the algebraic manipulations; it is, however, very minor.

[d] Weighted average of median earnings for occupational categories.

[e] Weighted average, with female frequencies applied to male median earnings.

[f] Weighted average, with male frequencies applied to female median earnings.

[g] The portion of the gap due to occupational segregation is computed two ways: (A) = [(3) − (4)/[(1) − (4)]; (B) = [(1) − (2)]/[(1) − (4)]. The portion of the gap due to within-occupation earnings differences is, of course, the complement of the portion due to occupational segregation.

SOURCE: U.S. Bureau of the Census, 1973:Table 1, and the "Occupational Characteristics Summary File" computer tape (see Treiman, 1973, for a description).

TABLE 10 Summary of Studies Accounting for Sex Differences in Earnings on the Basis of Worker Characteristics and Job Characteristics

| Author | Data Source and Population Studied | Measure of Earnings | Statistical Method and Explanatory Variables[a] | Women's Earnings as a Percentage of Men's | | Percentage of Gap Explained[a] |
|---|---|---|---|---|---|---|
| | | | | Observed | Adjusted | |
| *Representative national samples* | | | | | | |
| Featherman and Hauser | OCG:[e] Married, spouse-present men, 20–64 in ECLF and their wives | 1961, 1972 annual earnings | R, S: 1, 7, 10, 23 | 38 | 48 | 16 |
| Cohen | Survey of working conditions: Full-time wage and salary workers, age 22–64 | 1969 annual earnings | K, S: 1, 2, 10, 11, 16, 24, 27, 28 | 55 | 71 | 36 |
| Oaxaca | SEO:[f] Urban employees, age 16 + | 1967 hourly earnings | R, S: 1, 3, 7–10, 12, 13, 21, 25–27 | | | |
| Whites | | | | 65 | 78 | 37 |
| Blacks | | | | 67 | 80 | 39 |
| Roos | GSS[g] 1974–1977: Currently employed white men and women, 25–64 | Earnings from previous year | R, S: 1, 2, 10, 22, 23, 26, 29, 30, 31 | 46 | 63 | 31 |
| Sanborn | Census: Employed civilian wage and salary workers | 1949 annual earnings | F: 1–3, 10, 18, 20  F: 1–3, 6, 10, 16, 18, 19, 20, 24 | 58  58 | 76  88 | 43  71 |
| *National samples, restricted age* | | | | | | |
| Suter and Miller | NLS,[h] CPS:[i] Wage and salary workers, age 30–44 | 1966 annual earnings | R, S: 1, 6, 10, 23 | 39 | 62 | 38 |
| Treiman and Terrell | NLS:[h] Employed women age 30–44 and their husbands | 1966 annual earnings | R, S: 1, 6, 7, 10, 17, 22 | | | |
| Whites | | | | 42 | 67 | 43 |
| Nonwhites | | | | 54 | 68 | 30 |

[a] Statistical methods: F = frequency distribution or tabular standardization, R = regression analysis, S = separate equations for males and females.

Explanatory variables (see also Table 4):

1. Education
2. Age
3. Race
4. Mental ability (intelligence)
5. Formal training
6. Actual labor market experience
7. Proxy for labor market experience
8. Marital status
9. Health
10. Hours of work (annual, weekly, full-time/part-time)
11. Tenure (length of service with current employer)
12. Size of city of residence
13. Region of residence
14. SES background (parental education, occupation, income, number of siblings, migration history, ethnicity, etc.)
15. Quality of schooling
16. Absenteeism record
17. Dual burden (number of children, limits on hours or location, plans to stop work for non-training reasons, etc.)
18. Urban/rural
19. Turnover
20. Occupation (census 3-digit)
21. Occupation (census 1-digit)
22. Occupational prestige
23. Occupational SEI (Duncan scale)
24. Other occupational classification or scale
25. Class of worker (self-employed, government, or private wage and salary)
26. Industry
27. Union membership
28. Type of employer (government/private, sex segregated/integrated, size of work force)
29. Supervisory status
30. Percent female
31. Median income of male incumbents

[b] Average female earnings expressed as a percentage of average male earnings.

[c] Adjusted earnings indicate the ratio of female to male earnings if the two sexes had the same average levels (or composition) on the explanatory variables. When several adjustments are presented in the original study their average is shown here.

[d] This is given by (expected − observed)/(100 − observed).

[e] OCG = CPS survey of Occupational Changes in a Generation

[f] SEO = Survey of Economic Opportunity

[g] GSS = General Social Survey

[h] NLS = National Longitudinal Surveys (Parnes)

[i] CPS = Current Population Survey

across these more narrowly defined occupations that accounts for a large portion of the earnings gap. Sanborn's study, however, includes no variables that attempt to describe characteristics of jobs, and his study provides no information as to what it is about these occupations that accounts for earnings differences.

One study is particularly informative about the explanatory power of the different types of variables. Roos (1981) found that variables of the human capital type accounted for about 20 percent of the difference in earnings; that the addition of Duncan's socioeconomic index and prestige variables did not account for any additional portion, nor did occupational characteristics from the *Dictionary of Occupational Titles*; and that the addition of other occupational characteristics (industry, supervisory status, percent female, and median income of male incumbents) accounted for an additional 11 percent of the difference. Roos's occupational characteristics can be thought of as of two types, "benign" and "suspect," with respect to the issue of comparable worth. Benign characteristics, such as ratings of job complexity, supervisory duties, and possibly industry (which might stand for the ability of an employer to pay), are, like the productivity differences that human capital variables attempt to measure, generally regarded as legitimate bases for pay differentials. Suspect characteristics, such as percent female and median earnings of male incumbents, generally would not be considered legitimate because they indicate the extent to which women's lower earnings are related to their being in jobs held mainly by women and in low-paying jobs. Roos's study of determinants of individual earnings is consistent with the staff study reported above (Hartmann et al., 1980) on determinants of occupational earnings, which indicates that percent female is an important determinant of earnings.[21]

On the whole, however, the studies of earnings differences that use job characteristics as explanatory variables do not constitute a definitive body of literature. There are simply not enough of such studies nor are they conclusive enough to show what it is about jobs held mainly by

---

[21] In a different context, several studies by economists have related job characteristics to wages in an attempt to test the theory of compensating or equalizing wage differences originally suggested by Adam Smith. (The theory suggests that unpleasant job characteristics should earn a premium.) Lucas (1977), using job characteristics from the *Dictionary of Occupational Titles*, found, for example, that positive coefficients are estimated for variables representing repetitiveness and unpleasant physical working conditions, suggesting that they can be viewed as compensating differences. Robert Smith (1979) summarizes the generally mixed results of a number of these empirical studies. These studies can be viewed as attempts to estimate the implicit prices of job characteristics from knowledge of the explicit prices—the wage rates of jobs—and are thus an example of hedonic price equations of the type discussed by Rosen (1974).

men and those held mainly by women that accounts for their differences in earnings. These studies do confirm, however, the importance of job segregation by sex in explaining the difference in earnings between men and women.

Two kinds of detailed studies do provide a more complete understanding of the effect of job segregation on earnings: studies of particular occupational groups and studies of workers in individual firms or organizations. The fraction of the types of jobs covered by these studies is unknown. Still, they provide some sense of the extent and impact of job segregation on pay differentials by sex and by race.

First, for many, if not most, occupations a substantial portion of the difference in average earnings between men and women can be attributed to the fact that women are more likely than men to be employed in low-paying firms and less likely to be employed in high-paying firms. Blau's (1977) detailed study in three metropolitan labor markets of selected white-collar occupations filled by both men and women is particularly instructive on this point. Blau investigated the distribution of workers among firms and found that the job segregation of men and women is important in explaining wage differentials even when occupations are integrated. Using data provided by the Bureau of Labor Statistics, Blau demonstrates that within occupations that are integrated by sex, such as accounting clerk, men and women are not randomly distributed among firms: there is more segregation by sex across firms than would occur through random hiring processes. Moreover, a wage hierarchy exists among firms: those that employ more men in a given occupation than expected from a model of random hiring processes pay the highest wages, those that are integrated pay average wages, and those that employ more women than expected pay the lowest wages.[22]

Blau finds that more of the within-occupation wage differences between men and women can be explained by differences in pay among firms than can be explained by differences in pay within firms. That is, the wage hierarchy among firms and the segregation of women into the low-wage firms account for the larger part of the differential in men's and women's wages. Blau finds that this wage hierarchy is consistent across occupations, so that those firms that pay higher wages do so in all of the occupations studied. Moreover, firms at the high end of the hierarchy hire fewer women across all occupations.

These results lend support to an institutional explanation for wage differentials. Since Blau's study does not rely on particular attributes

---

[22] These findings are similar to those reported by Buckley (1971) for eight office and two plant occupations, each with significant numbers of job-holders of both sexes, as well as those reported by McNulty (1967).

of occupations to explain either differentials in pay or segregation itself, it points to those structural and institutional factors that can affect all jobs. Since the occupations she studied are very narrowly defined, they must have similar attributes regardless of whether they are performed by men or women, and the incumbents are likely to have similar qualifications and experience. Occupational segregation by sex exists nevertheless. A number of other studies have also shown that within occupations jobs are substantially segregated across firms, always with the result that jobs held mainly by men are paid more than jobs held mainly by women.[23]

Occupational segregation also exists within firms and is widely known to be common, although precise measurement of its extent is difficult because publicly available data at the establishment level are rare. To a large extent, the occupational segregation observed within firms simply mirrors that observed in the labor market as a whole. For example, the secretaries that firms hire are primarily women because most trained secretaries are women; similarly, the accountants they hire are primarily men because most trained accountants are men.

In many firms it is typical for managerial jobs to be dominated by white men; for professional jobs to be dominated by whites, although not so exclusively by white men as managerial positions; for clerical jobs to be dominated by women; for craft and laboring jobs to be dominated by men; for specific operative jobs to be dominated by one sex or the other and sometimes by one race or ethnic group; and for most service jobs to be dominated by women and minority men.

An interesting example comes from the U.S. Office of Personnel Management (formerly the U.S. Civil Service Commission), which determines personnel policies for the federal government, the nation's largest single employer of white-collar workers. The Office of Personnel Management uses a standardized occupational grading system (the "General Schedule," GS) consisting of 18 grades defined on the basis of the knowledge required for a position, the degree of autonomy, and a number of other factors (see Treiman, 1979:17–20, for a more detailed description). A GS level is assigned to each job in the federal civil service, which determines its pay range; hence, the GS hierarchy is also a pay hierarchy. Table 11 shows the distribution of federal white-collar workers by GS level and sex as of November 1977. Women are over-

---

[23] See, for example, Bridges and Berk's study (1974) of nonsupervisory white-collar employees in Chicago-area financial institutions; Talbert and Bose's study (1977) of retail clerks in a metropolitan area; Allison's study (1976) of beauty salon operators; and the study by Darland et al. (1974) of salary differences between male and female college and university faculty.

TABLE 11   Percent Female by Occupational Grade (GS Level) in the Federal Civil Service for Full-Time, White-Collar Employees of Federal Government Agencies, 1977

| GS Level | Percentage Female | Percentage Distribution of All Employees |
|---|---|---|
| 16–18 | 3 | a |
| 14–15 | 5 | 6 |
| 12–13 | 10 | 19 |
| 9–11 | 30 | 24 |
| 5–8 | 63 | 30 |
| 1–4 | 77 | 20 |
| TOTAL | 43 | 100 |
| N | (615,342) | (1,429,645) |

a Less than 0.5 percent.

SOURCE: Barrett, 1979:Table 4.

whelmingly concentrated in the lower grades, in what are, for the most part, clerical jobs (see also Osterman's 1978 study of a large publishing firm).

Job segregation by sex, whether within a firm or across firms, provides an important clue to the causes of the difference in earnings between women and men, yet leaves open the question of why jobs and occupations are segregated and what the exact relationship is between job segregation and pay differentials. While it is clear that women are concentrated in jobs that pay less, it is unclear to what extent this is because women choose jobs with low pay for reasons other than their sex composition (for example, because they tend not to penalize incumbents with intermittent labor force experience), to what extent women are restricted to such jobs, and to what extent some jobs pay less than others *because* they tend to be held by women. We take up these questions in the next chapter.

## CONCLUSION

In this chapter we have reviewed evidence on the extent and causes of earnings differentials between men and women. That such differentials exist is not in dispute: among full-time year-round workers the earnings of women average less than 60 percent of those of men. What causes the difference in earnings is a matter of considerable dispute. The evidence suggests, however, that only a small part of the earnings

differences between men and women can be accounted for by differences
in education, labor force experience, labor force commitment, or other
human capital factors believed to contribute to productivity differences
among workers. The findings from studies attempting to explain the
differences in earnings between men and women on the basis of such
factors usually account for less than a quarter and never more than half
of the observed earnings differences.

The evidence reviewed on job segregation by sex suggests that an
additional part of the earnings gap results from the fact that women are
concentrated in low-paying jobs. Job segregation by sex is quite pronounced and shows few signs of substantially diminishing. Women are
concentrated in low-paying occupations and, within occupations, in low-
paying firms. The significant degree of job segregation by sex may be
a consequence of a variety of institutional forces, discriminatory practices, or other factors that operate in the labor market to depress market
wage rates for women's jobs. In Chapter 3 we investigate the institutional features of the U.S. labor market that may depress women's wages
and result in the persistence of an earnings differential between men
and women over time.

## TECHNICAL NOTE

Two logically similar statistical methods have been used in human
capital studies of sex discrimination in earnings, sometimes in combination: demographic standardization techniques and decomposition procedures based on multiple-regression analysis. Since the latter are more
common, we describe them in some detail.

Let us consider a hypothetical regression analysis of the difference in
the earnings of men and women. The conventional approach is to estimate, separately for men and women, an ordinary least-squares regression equation of the form

$$Y = a + \Sigma b_i X_i \,, \tag{1}$$

where $Y$ is the worker's earnings and the $X_i$ are the worker's human
capital characteristics (e.g., years of school completed, years of labor
force experience, amount of on-the-job training). First the equations
are estimated for each sex; then the mean values of each of the human
capital characteristics (the $X_i$) for one sex are substituted in the equation
estimated for the other sex to derive an estimate of the average earnings
expected if the only difference in average earnings between men and

women was due to differences in the measured human capital characteristics.

For example, suppose that for a sample of men the least-squares estimate of earnings from schooling and experience is

$$\hat{Y} = 1,000 + 500(\text{years of schooling}) + 200(\text{years of experience}) \quad (2)$$

and that their average level of earnings is $10,000, that their average amount of schooling is 10 years, and that they have an average of 20 years of labor force experience. Now, suppose further that the average level of earnings of women is $6,000, that their average amount of schooling is 11 years, and that they have an average of 10 years of labor force experience. Substituting the means for women into the equation for men (eq. 2),

$$Y = 1,000 + 500(11) + 200(10) = 8,500, \quad (3)$$

which implies that if women had the same rate of return on their education and experience as men they would earn 85 percent (8,500/10,000) as much as men, while in this example (and in the U.S. economy) women actually earn only 60 percent as much as men. On this basis, the total earnings gap is decomposed into a portion due to differences in human capital factors and a portion due to differences in rates of return on those factors. In this example, about two-thirds of the earnings gap ([85 − 60]/[100 − 60]) could be attributed to the fact that women get a lower return on their education and experience and about one-third of the earnings gap to differences between men and women in the amount of their education and experience. Alternatively, the means for men on education and experience could be substituted into an equation for women. This does not usually produce an identical answer, but the two sets of answers tend to be similar (see Oaxaca, 1973, for a discussion of this issue, known as the index problem).

Usually the difference in rates of return estimated from such equations (that is, the difference remaining after gender differences in the factors thought to affect productivity have been controlled) is taken to represent discrimination. This approach has a number of difficulties, which are discussed above.

# 3 Wage Differentials and Institutional Features of Labor Markets

What features of the wage-setting process create the differences in wages observed between men and women and between minorities and nonminorities? What explains the extent of job segregation observed? Why do these differences persist? In this chapter we take an institutional view of labor markets in examining these questions, and we argue that it is likely that some portion of the wage differentials observed can be regarded as the result of discrimination, both intentional and unintentional. In reviewing a variety of explanations for the existence of discrimination offered by economists, we note that none of them satisfactorily explains the causes of discrimination, but each suggests that it is plausible that discrimination exists. Finally, we briefly consider the implications of the complexity of labor markets for implementing policies to reduce discrimination and its effects.

## LABOR MARKETS

Of today's employed civilian labor force of approximately 100 million, about 90 percent work for wages or salaries (the rest are self-employed). For employees, access to jobs, wage levels, conditions of work, and other aspects of employment are determined by the operation of labor markets. In the conventional model of perfectly competitive labor markets, demanders and suppliers of labor possess complete information and total mobility; the bargaining of individual employees and employers and the unfettered adjustment of supply and demand determine the

wage of each worker; consequently, the wage of each worker exactly
equals the value of his or her economic contribution (i.e., marginal
revenue product). But workers rarely participate in the labor market
with full information or mobility, are often not aware of all opportunities, and are not likely to have access to all of them (Rees and Schultz,
1970). Similarly, employers rarely have access to all possible employees
and are often constrained by custom, agreements, and other factors.
Major institutional constraints include internal labor markets (arrangements in which most positions are filled by promotion from within a
firm); union agreements that determine hiring rules and pay rates; and
the segmentation of labor markets into noncompeting groups, largely
on the basis of the sex, race, and ethnicity of workers. While institutional
economists acknowledge that wage rates observed in the market reflect
the forces of supply and demand, they point out that supply and demand
are themselves strongly affected by institutional factors. In this view,
rigidities and barriers to mobility characterize labor markets, and inequalities in wages between workers with similar qualifications doing
similar work are endemic.

Institutional analysis differs from the more conventional neoclassical
analysis of the operation of labor markets in its emphasis on the importance of institutional features and their relative inflexibility in determining wages and other conditions of employment. In the judgment
of the committee, the institutional view offers a more fruitful perspective
from which to understand the existence and the persistence of wage
differentials between men and women, especially since, as we note in
Chapter 2, attempts to explain earnings differences by productivity differences have not been very successful. Our discussion, which focuses
on institutional features, should not, however, be interpreted as a comprehensive review of all approaches to understanding the operation of
labor markets. The institutional view is only one view of labor markets,
and is the subject of much controversy currently in economics and sociology (Doeringer and Piore, 1971; Wachter, 1975; Cain, 1976; Beck
et al., 1978; Piore, 1979; Hauser, 1980; England, 1982).

## COMPARABLE WORTH AND INTERNAL LABOR MARKETS

Issues involving the comparable worth of jobs emerge most clearly
and acutely in situations in which a single firm employs a large work
force allocated among many different types of jobs. Such situations are
fairly common, since at least half of the U.S. work force is employed
by large-scale employers: 20 percent of all wage workers are employed

by federal, state, and local governments, and 40 percent (nearly half of those in the private sector) work in private establishments that employ 100 or more workers (U.S. Bureau of the Census, 1979:xxiii). The 500 largest industrial corporations (the *Fortune* 500) alone employed 16 million workers in 1979, about 45 percent of all workers in manufacturing and mining, averaging about 32,000 workers per company. The largest U.S. industrial employer, General Motors, has more than 800,000 employees, and the largest nonindustrial employer, American Telephone and Telegraph, has about 1 million employees.

For most of these workers the conditions of employment are determined largely by administrative rules, promulgated by employers or negotiated by employers and unions (about a quarter of all U.S. nonagricultural workers are members of unions). Once an employee enters a large-scale establishment, he or she becomes part of an "internal" labor market in which job openings are usually filled from within and workers are usually deployed in accordance with established rules and procedures rather than in direct competition with workers in the "external" labor market. For many workers, movement into (and between) large firms with highly organized internal labor markets is quite limited (Doeringer and Piore, 1971; Edwards, 1979).

Several theories seek to explain why internal labor markets are created. Doeringer and Piore (1971) argue that because modern technologies require specificity of skills and relatively long periods of on-the-job training at the employer's expense, employers attempt to minimize turnover and enhance the stability of the labor force by creating job structures within firms that reward longevity—such as increments based on seniority and promotions up well-defined job ladders. Economic forces operate on employers, of course, but they operate mainly to encourage employers to minimize their training costs by minimizing turnover. Thurow (1975) suggests that higher wages are needed to "bribe" older workers to teach their skills to younger ones. Gordon (1972) and Stone (1975) suggest that the existence of many different job ladders, each with several rungs, may not be required by differences in skill levels but instead may serve to divide workers (particularly by race, ethnicity, or sex), thus minimizing the collective power of the workers and enhancing that of the employer. Edwards (1979) argues that management creates internal job structures primarily in order to provide incentives for workers to perform their jobs, rather than because of skill requirements. Kahn (1976) provides an example of a union taking the lead role in transforming a capricious, casual labor market in longshoring into a highly structured one, primarily to reap such benefits as higher wages, seniority increases, and employment stability.

According to all these explanations, job structures that entail many rungs on a long ladder, each step requiring greater skill or involving more pay and responsibility, are established. Only for entry-level jobs are wage rates strongly influenced by the competitive forces of supply and demand. The major supply for the jobs higher on the ladder are those workers already in the firm, and the only effective demand for those particular workers is that of their current employer. Some of the jobs have few, if any, analogues in the external labor market and no established market wage rates; rather it is the employer, and possibly workers, who determine appropriate wage rates for the jobs.

If internally organized jobs were directly open to external market competition, employers would find little use for extensive compensation analysis (except perhaps for area wage surveys to determine the "going wage"). The fact that many large firms use such analyses, particularly job evaluation, to link internal jobs to particular "benchmark" jobs—jobs that do have external markets and external wage rates (Treiman, 1979)—supports the notion that, within broad limits, such jobs are shielded from immediate external competition. Additional sources of institutional rigidity arise from the prevalence of custom and tradition in setting wages (see, for example, Phelps-Brown, 1977; Wootton, 1955) and the relative immobility of workers between firms. Since access to higher-paying jobs comes only from within a firm, workers stand to benefit by remaining with that firm, generally do not seek jobs elsewhere, and may be unaware of other opportunities.

## SEGMENTATION OF THE LABOR MARKET

The existence of internal labor markets and other institutional features has led some researchers to the concept of labor market segmentation. The part of the economy characterized by highly articulated internal labor markets is called the primary segment. It consists of industries with advanced technology, large capital investments, unionization, sometimes a degree of insulation from competition in their product markets, or high profits—industries such as petroleum, chemicals, heavy equipment manufacture, and utilities (Bluestone, 1970; Doeringer and Piore, 1971; Edwards, 1979). Industries that require highly educated workers, such as computer manufacture and service, insurance, and finance as well as most of the public service sector, also tend to have well-developed internal labor markets with established channels for advancement and predictable work rules and hence are also part of the primary segment.

The remaining jobs in the economy constitute what has been called the secondary segment. These jobs have little insulation from competitive market pressures and more closely approximate the textbook model of a perfect market. In addition, they generally tend to have "low wages and fringe benefits, poor working conditions, high labor turnover, little chance of advancement, and often arbitrary and capricious supervision" (Doeringer and Piore, 1971:165). Such jobs tend to be found in highly competitive industries with low capital investment, little unionization, and low profits—many service-oriented industries and such manufacturing industries as textiles, garment making, and food processing (Bluestone et al., 1973; Tyler, 1978). The secondary segment includes many jobs requiring relatively little job-specific skill—attendant, guard, food server, sales clerk, stock clerk, messenger, and cleaning worker; seasonal jobs, particularly in agriculture; and increasing numbers of clerical jobs in typing, filing, and keypunching pools. For all these jobs, the most salient distinguishing feature is the relative insecurity or lack of an internal market structure—that is, the immediacy with which these jobs are subject to external market forces (Edwards, 1979).

Although primary jobs are thought to prevail in large firms and industries with a historical pattern of structured internal labor markets, and secondary jobs to prevail in enterprises with no formal internal labor markets, both types of jobs may exist side by side. For example, service jobs in hospitals exist alongside medical and nursing jobs; and janitorial and packaging jobs in large firms exist alongside skilled craft jobs. But in neither case do the secondary jobs feed into job ladders leading to the primary jobs.

Jobs traditionally held by women—teaching, nursing, and secretarial work—have some features of organization that are more characteristic of a secondary than a primary pattern. Despite relatively high levels of skill, the wage levels of these jobs are often low. For example, in 1976 in manufacturing industries sampled by the Bureau of Labor Statistics, 12 of 26 clerical occupations were paid less than janitors (Ward, 1980). Jobs traditionally held by women often have short job ladders. It has been noted that these jobs often involve generalizable skills that can be moved from one job to another, the acquisition of which is paid for by women themselves (Oppenheimer, 1970). One plausible explanation of these attributes is that they have evolved because employers, believing women to have short job tenure and high turnover rates, have been unwilling to bear large training costs or to structure these jobs in such a way as to make their investments in training pay off in greater longevity.[1]

---

[1] Other job structures for these occupations are possible. Secretarial work, for example, could be organized as a skilled craft with apprenticeships, entry-level jobs, and career ladders, particularly when firm-specific skills are important.

TABLE 12  Distribution of Earnings in Selected Occupations in the Newark Metropolitan Area, January 1980

| Occupation | Earnings[a] | |
|---|---|---|
| | Median | Range[b] |
| | Hourly, Straight Time | |
| Electricians, maintenance | $8.63 | $6.40–14.00 |
| Mechanics, maintenance (automotive) | 9.05 | 5.60–11.80 |
| Tool- and diemakers | 8.78 | 6.00–11.80 |
| Forklift operators | 6.69 | 3.50–9.30 |
| Order fillers | 4.85 | 3.30–8.90 |
| | Weekly, Straight Time | |
| Stenographers, senior | $250.50 | $140.00–340.00 |
| Secretaries, class A | 328.00 | 200.00–460.00 |
| Key entry operators, class B | 180.00 | 120.00–340.00 |
| Draftsmen, class A | 379.50 | 260.00–600.00 |
| Computer programmers (business) class A | 352.00 | 240.00–600.00 |
| Registered industrial nurses | 291.50 | 180.00–480.00 |

[a] Exclusive of premium pay for overtime and for work on weekends, holidays, and late shifts.
[b] The lowest and highest rates received by the workers surveyed.

SOURCE: U.S. Department of Labor, Bureau of Labor Statistics, 1980a.

In contrast, it has been claimed that employers respond to the possibility of men leaving their jobs after costly training has been invested in them by structuring the jobs in such a way as to discourage turnover and reward longevity. The consequence of this difference in the way "women's" and "men's" jobs are usually structured is that jobs that traditionally have been held by women often have more exposure to marketplace competition and provide less advancement with seniority and experience than jobs that traditionally have been held by men.

Although institutional theorists disagree about some of the causes, a sizable (and growing) empirical literature presents a fairly consistent picture of labor market segmentation.[2] That *jobs* are segmented—not only *occupations*—is indicated by the range of wages paid for very similar work, a phenomenon that has been well known for some time (Wootton, 1955; Chamberlain and Cullen, 1971). Table 12 shows considerable variation in a sample of occupational wage rates paid by surveyed establishments in one metropolitan area, Newark, New Jersey. For this sam-

[2] The following summary of the empirical literature on labor market segmentation relies heavily on Edwards (1979).

ple the highest-paid workers generally received more than twice as much
as the lowest-paid workers in the same narrowly defined occupations.
Other research confirms the existence of high-wage and low-wage firms
that tend to pay consistently high or low wages to all employees (Rees
and Schultz, 1970; Blau, 1977; Ward, 1980). This wide variation in wages
reflects an underlying structure of segmented labor markets.

Early research posited the existence of segmented labor markets.
Doeringer and Piore (1971) found through extensive interviewing that
decisions about hiring, pay, and termination are made in very different
ways in the primary and secondary segments, the secondary segment
being characterized by arbitrariness and the primary segment by systematic procedures. Several historical studies suggest that in job search
processes, workers in the secondary segment, particularly minority
workers, have been restricted by lack of information and in many cases
by discrimination in access by employers. Minority workers in particular
often perceive that only a narrow set of jobs is open to them, and they
use very limited community networks to find jobs (Baron and Hymer,
1968; Baron, 1971; Glenn, 1980).

The appropriate way to define labor market segments quantitatively
is a matter of considerable debate. Theory suggests that they should be
defined by such characteristics as occupation, industry, stability, autonomy, unionization, and advancement opportunity. In practice, information on all these relevant characteristics is rarely available in most
data sets, and researchers use various, not wholly satisfactory, indicators
(such as wage rates and industry or occupation alone). One estimate
suggests that roughly a quarter of the U.S. labor force hold jobs in the
secondary segment and slightly more than half hold jobs in the primary
segment—divided into an independent primary segment (25 percent)
and a subordinate primary segment (30 percent). About 20 percent of
the labor force (e.g., self-employed persons, high-level managers) fall
outside the schema (Edwards, 1979:166).

The empirical literature further suggests that various labor market
processes operate differently in the two segments, although Cain (1976)
has questioned the validity of findings of differences between segments
when the findings relate to variables that are correlated with, or the
same as, those used to define the segments.[3] Several empirical studies
suggest that training, mobility, schooling, and seniority have different
payoffs in terms of wages in the different segments (Buchele, 1976;
Rumberger and Carnoy, 1980). Wages in the secondary segment typi-

---

[3] This criticism is not applicable to Buchele's study (1976), which uses job content
variables as the basis for defining the segments, then proceeds to investigate the wage-
setting process.

cally average 70 to 75 percent of those in the primary segment. Job tenure and employment stability are also less certain in secondary jobs. Earnings equations, like those based on human capital models, suggest that the returns to years of schooling and experience are virtually zero in the secondary segment (Edwards, 1979:168–69). In the primary segment, by contrast, returns to schooling and experience are generally substantial, at least for men. Osterman found that the earnings of men in the independent primary segment increased 34 percent for each 10 years' additional experience; the earnings of those in the subordinate primary segment increased 18 percent; and the earnings of those in the secondary segment increased only 4 percent (Edwards, 1979:175). Osterman (1978) also found that each year of schooling increased a man's earnings by 10 percent in the independent primary segment, 6 percent in the subordinate primary segment, and only 1.5 percent in the secondary segment (Edwards, 1979:175). Similar differences have also been found by Buchele (1976) and Rumberger and Carnoy (1980).

Such findings are consistent with the hypothesis that different labor market segments operate in different ways, but they are at odds with the general tenor of the neoclassical human capital model of the labor market. Neoclassical theorists recognize "transitional" phenomena that result in the labor market's being out of equilibrium. For example, computer personnel are "overpaid" until enough workers can train for the position; workers in new oil fields are "overpaid" until more workers arrive. Moreover, jobs in rural areas may remain at slightly lower wage levels than urban jobs because the difference in wage levels is not great enough to overcome the costs of search and relocation. "Equalizing" or "compensating" wage differentials are also recognized by neoclassical theorists: risky, dirty, or unpleasant jobs are thought to earn premiums (relative to others requiring similar skills) in order to induce workers to take them. Jobs that require long and costly training also command such premiums (Friedman, 1971; Robert Smith, 1979). The neoclassical view recognizes the existence of noncompeting groups (men and women, for example) in the labor market, but their existence is seen as an anomaly, expected to disappear over time due to the forces of competition. The difference between the neoclassical and institutional views thus turns on judgments regarding the importance and systematic nature of market imperfections, not their presence or absence. In the institutional view, such imperfections are seen to be logical outcomes of product and labor market processes, so large and so pervasive that they dominate the wage-setting process.

In the institutional analysis, a worker's marginal productivity or worth to the employer is determined not only by the human capital he or she brings to the market but also by the way his or her job is structured.

The institutional approach considers as influences in the determination of wages such factors as the structure of the product market of employers, the arrangement of jobs by employers, unionization, capital intensity, and technological factors, in addition to human capital attributes. What a job is "worth" to an employer depends largely on how the employer chooses to structure it (given the constraints of industry, profit margins, and so forth) as well as on the customs and traditions of the particular workplace. Workers do not operate as individuals in the labor market, but rather as members of groups defined by their relationship to labor market structures, and labor market structures effectively limit the choices open to them: "Over significantly long periods, job structures exist, and workers must live with them as best they can" (Harrison and Sum, 1979:694).

## JOB SEGREGATION

Job segregation by sex, race, and ethnicity is common in today's labor market. Women and men and minorities and nonminorities often work in different jobs. As Blau (1977) has demonstrated for several narrowly defined clerical occupations, even for occupations that are integrated by sex, men and women work in different firms, with men more likely to be found in high-wage firms and industries. Hence, even when occupations are integrated by sex, the jobs men and women actually hold are segregated by sex.[4] Because custom and tradition have in the past assigned subordinate social roles to minorities and women and because labor markets tend to incorporate, mirror, and perpetuate such roles, institutional theorists would expect minorities and women to hold low-paying jobs with limited opportunities. As we concluded in Chapter 2, the evidence on the differences in earnings between men and women suggests both that they cannot be satisfactorily accounted for on the basis of worker characteristics thought to affect productivity and that job segregation contributes to the lower earnings of women. Why women are concentrated in low-paying jobs is a crucial question still left unresolved. Three different explanations have been offered: women choose, for reasons other than pay, jobs that turn out to pay poorly; women are excluded from high-paying jobs; and the jobs that women hold tend to be underpaid because they are held by women. If the latter two explanations have empirical support, we must conclude that employment discrimination and wage discrimination exist.

[4] Beck et al. (1978, 1980a, 1980b) have reported empirical findings on women's work and earnings in segmented labor markets (see Hauser, 1980, for a critique); for earlier work on women in low-wage industries, see Stevenson (1973, 1974, 1975); for a historical treatment, see Hartmann (1976).

CHOICE

It is sometimes asserted that women choose to work at certain types of jobs despite the fact that such jobs have relatively low pay rates. A variety of reasons has been offered. First, women may be socialized to believe that some types of jobs are appropriate and that others are inappropriate for women; socialization may be so effective for some women that it never even occurs to them to consider other types of jobs. Second, women may have pursued courses of study they thought particularly appropriate to women and in consequence may not have the education or training that would suit them for other available jobs. Third, women may lack information about other available jobs, their pay rates, working conditions, and access to them. Fourth, women may be aware of alternatives, but because of actual or expected family obligations may structure their labor force participation in particular ways. For example, they may be unwilling to invest a great deal of time, effort, or money in preparing for jobs because they do not expect to remain in the labor force after marriage or after childbearing. They may be willing to accept low-paying jobs, or jobs with limited opportunities for advancement, and hold them until they marry and begin to raise children. Or, in expectation of returning to work after their children are in school or grown, they may choose jobs that are easy to leave and reenter, jobs that do not require the continuous accumulation of skills and consequently do not lead to significant increases in earnings with experience (Mincer and Polachek, 1974, 1978; Polachek, 1976, 1979). To accommodate the dual demands of work and family responsibilities, women may choose jobs with limited demands—restricted hours, no overtime work, no travel requirements, etc. Or they may defer to the demands of their husbands' career advancement, moving with their husbands from place to place, etc. (Oppenheimer, 1970). Some of these family-related factors may influence women's willingness to pursue advancement in their jobs. Fifth, women may be aware of alternative types of jobs but believe them to be unavailable or unpleasant because of discrimination; their labor market preparation and behavior may be affected in many ways by this perception: the course of study they take; the time, money, and effort invested in training; their willingness to accept promotion, etc.

It is difficult to assess the relative importance of the choices women make in the labor market and of the factors affecting their choices.[5]

---

[5] An extensive literature exists on some of the relevant topics, especially socialization. For useful reviews see Maccoby and Jacklin (1974), Mednick et al. (1975), Scanzoni (1975), Duncan and Duncan (1978), and Laws (1979); for bibliographies of these materials see Astin et al. (1971), Bickner (1974), and Astin et al. (1975).

Many of these "choices" are adaptations to constraints of various kinds. Others are the result of complex social-psychological processes. Women's choices observed so far may change (and may already be undergoing change) as women's participation in the labor market changes. More and more women are entering the labor market and remaining in it even when their children are very young.[6] Their career expectations, their willingness to invest in training, and so on may be affected by these changes.

When efforts have been made to measure these factors, in an attempt to explain the difference in earnings between women and men, the results have been mixed. Using data on women ages 30–44 from the National Longitudinal Study (NLS), Mincer and Polachek (1974) found that wages varied positively with work experience and negatively with work interruption, and they estimated that half the earnings gap between men and women could be accounted for by their different patterns of labor force participation. They reasoned that work interruptions would be important because women's skills would depreciate while they were out of the labor market.

Polachek (1976, 1979) has suggested that women choose jobs the wages of which will be least affected by interruptions (because such jobs have low returns on experience). Using data for women of all ages from the Panel Study of Income Dynamics, however, Corcoran (1979) found that continuity of work experience did not seem to have a large effect on earnings differentials between men and women, and, in particular, that labor force withdrawals did not usually lower women's wages— their skills did not in general atrophy or depreciate while they were out of the labor market. England (1982), using the NLS data for women ages 30–44, attempted to test the Polachek thesis by estimating the amount of skill depreciation that women with intermittent labor force participation experience in different occupations. She found no correlation between rates of skill depreciation and the percent female in occupations, indicating that women probably do not choose their occupations to minimize income loss, as Polachek suggests.

---

[6] In recent years, the largest proportional increase in labor force participation has been among married women: in 1947, married women's participation rate was 20 percent; by 1979, nearly 48 percent of all married women were working outside the home (Ralph E. Smith, 1979:4). Moreover, much of this increase involves the increasing participation of women traditionally least likely to work—married women living with their husbands and with young children. In 1950, 11.9 percent of married women with husbands and with children under six years old were employed; by 1980, about 45 percent were employed (U.S. Department of Labor, Bureau of Labor Statistics, 1977:Tables 18 and 22; Bureau of Labor Statistics news release 80–767, Dec. 9, 1980).

EXCLUSION

A second explanation of why women are concentrated in low-paying jobs may be that they are simply excluded from high-paying jobs. While this needs to be established on a case-by-case basis, there are now a large number of documented cases of denial of occupational opportunities on the basis of sex (Schlei and Grossman, 1976). Historically, women were prohibited from certain jobs by laws designed to protect them from exploitation (see U.S. Department of Labor, Women's Bureau, 1969). More recently, in several major cases the courts found that women were excluded from higher-level or higher-paying jobs (EEOC, 1972; Osterman, 1978). Such exclusion may take the form of denial of employment or of restriction in opportunities for promotion.

While it is difficult to establish discriminatory intent on the part of employers, it is possible to study the pattern of employment within firms to determine whether men and women are allocated to jobs in a manner consistent with their qualifications. A study by Malkiel and Malkiel (1973) does this. Using data on professional employees of a large corporation, they showed that adjusting earnings on the basis of a very good measure of job-related labor market experience plus measures of post-high-school education, rate of absenteeism, marital status, college field of study, and personal productivity (measured by number of publications) increased the female/male earnings ratio from 66 percent to beween 75 and 89 percent (depending on the year and type of decomposition used). Adding a 13-category index of job level to the regression resulted in an adjusted earnings ratio of almost 1.0 (98 percent), which led the authors to conclude that in this firm there was no discrimination in the form of unequal pay for equal work but that there was discrimination in occupational assignment—specifically, that women were assigned to lower-level jobs than men with the same qualifications.

Studies by Talbert and Bose (1977) and Halaby (1979) also conclude that the lower wages of women result from discrimination. Talbert and Bose found that among retail sales clerks, men are more likely to be assigned to "big ticket" departments (furniture, large appliances, etc.) and hence to earn more. Halaby, using 1960 data for managerial personnel of a very large California-based public utility firm,[7] found that female managers earned about two-thirds of what male managers earned and that adjustments for differences between them with respect to education, seniority, previous labor force experience, and number of pre-

[7] "Managerial personnel" according to the company definition includes all supervisory personnel. Hence, the sample includes some individuals who would fall into the clerical and manual categories of the U.S. census classification.

TABLE 13   Decomposition of Earnings Differentials of Men and
Women Among Managerial Personnel in a Large Public Utility
Company

| Component | Percentage | Dollars |
|---|---|---|
| Human capital | | |
| Differences in mean levels | 5.7 | 155 |
| Differences in rate of return | 17.1 | 466 |
| Shared | − .7 | − 19 |
| TOTAL | 22.1 | 602 |
| Position structure | | |
| Differences in job composition | 43.8 | 1,194 |
| Differences in rank | 34.1 | 930 |
| TOTAL | 77.9 | 2,124 |
| TOTAL ALL SOURCES | 100.0 | 2,726 |

SOURCE: Adapted from Halaby, 1979:Table 9.

vious employers accounted for only about 13 percent of the difference
in earnings. At any given level of human capital, according to Halaby's
formulation, women tend to be concentrated in lower-level occupations
in the firm's hierarchy and at lower ranks within occupations, at substantial detriment to their earnings. Table 13 gives Halaby's decomposition of the total difference in earnings between men and women
into portions due to what he considers human capital variables and what
he considers job-related factors. More than 20 percent of the difference
is due to human capital variables, holding constant jobs and ranks: most
of that difference occurs because women get a lower return on these
human capital variables than men do; only about 5 percent of the difference occurs because women and men differ in their average levels
of human capital. The rest of the earnings gap arises from the fact that
women have lower-level positions when human capital is held constant.

UNDERPAYMENT OF WOMEN'S WORK

The third explanation for the lower pay rates of jobs held mainly by
women is that women's work is underpaid because women do it—that
is, that the same work would be paid more if it were done by men.
Again, the evidence is sparse, but in several documented cases pay rates
were shown to have been influenced by the sex composition of the work
force as well as by the content of jobs. The evidence consists of a
demonstration that employers violated their own criteria for determining

the relative monetary worth of jobs, in order either to implement an explicit decision to pay women or minority workers less than men or whites or to conform to an external standard for establishing pay rates. In both cases the evidence comes from an examination of the job evaluation procedures used by employers.

Job evaluation procedures, which are discussed more fully in Chapter 4 and also in the committee's interim report (Treiman, 1979), involve rating a group of jobs with respect to a set of "compensable factors," features of jobs that an employer regards as important in setting pay rates. Compensable factors usually include indicators of the skill, effort, and responsibility required by a job and the nature of the working conditions involved. In most firms that use job evaluation procedures the sum of scores on the set of rated factors is used to assign jobs to pay classes. In this context we would regard jobs held mainly or entirely by women as underpaid if their pay rates are lower than those of jobs with the same scores held mainly or entirely by men.

Several examples exist of firms that pay, or have paid, jobs held mainly by women less than jobs with similar job evaluation scores held mainly by men. Some of these pay practices antedate the passage of the 1963 Equal Pay Act and the 1964 Civil Rights Act; they were not illegal then and were in fact widely accepted. Such pay practices would be of historical interest only but for the fact that, in many cases, they continue to govern pay differences between jobs. For example, in 1945 the War Labor Board found, and the companies agreed, that both the Westinghouse Electric Corporation and the General Electric Company had reduced the pay rates of production jobs held by women to a level below those of jobs held by men—Westinghouse by 18–20 percent, General Electric by about 33 percent—even though the jobs had similar job evaluation scores (Newman, 1976).

In the late 1930s, General Electric and Westinghouse had established job evaluation systems for the purpose of standardizing wage rates throughout their plants. Most of the production jobs were entirely segregated by sex during this period and were known as either female or male jobs. At one Westinghouse plant, female jobs were assigned to five labor grades, 1 through 5; male jobs with the same job evaluation scores as the female jobs were assigned to parallel labor grades, 1 through 5; and five additional labor grades were specified for male jobs with higher scores (see Table 14). The wage rates for these male and female labor grades were not, however, parallel. In fact, the hourly wage rates were established in such a way as to pay all of the female labor grades less than the lowest male labor grade, despite the fact that the parallel male and female grades represented jobs of comparable

TABLE 14   Wage Rates at a Westinghouse Plant, 1943

| Labor Grade | Proba-tionary Rate | Qualify-ing Rate | Standard Rate | Evalua-tion Point Range |
|---|---|---|---|---|
| Female |  |  |  |  |
| 1 | $0.615 | $0.645 | $0.675 | 0–49 |
| 2 | 0.645 | 0.675 | 0.705 | 50–62 |
| 3 | 0.675 | 0.705 | 0.735 | 63–78 |
| 4 | 0.705 | 0.735 | 0.765 | 79–98 |
| 5 | 0.735 | 0.765 | 0.795 | 99–125 |
| Male |  |  |  |  |
| Common labor | — | — | $0.785 | 0–37 |
| 1 (6) | $0.785 | $0.785 | 0.815 | 38–49 |
| 2 (7) | 0.785 | 0.815 | 0.845 | 50–62 |
| 3 (8) | 0.815 | 0.845 | 0.875 | 63–78 |
| 4 (9) | 0.845 | 0.875 | 0.905 | 79–98 |
| 5 (10) | 0.875 | 0.905 | 0.955 | 99–123 |
| 6 (11) | 0.905 | 0.955 | 1.055 | 124–154 |
| 7 (12) | 0.955 | 1.055 | 1.055 | 155–199 |
| 8 (13) | 1.055 | 1.055 | 1.155 | 199–239 |
| 9 (14) | 1.055 | 1.155 | 1.255 | 240–299 |
| 10 (15) | 1.155 | 1.255 | 1.405 | 300 |

SOURCE: Adapted from Newman, 1976:268.

worth according to the company's own criteria. Only the male common labor classification paid less than the highest paid women's jobs. This rank ordering of labor grades and pay differentials remained essentially unchanged until the separate series for male and female jobs were abolished in 1965. When these separate series were merged into a single series in 1965, however, the male grades 1 through 10 were simply relabeled 6 through 15, so that the sex differential in pay was preserved. The labor grades were not combined in such a way as to reflect the original evaluation of these jobs.

A similar situation existed at several General Electric Company plants. As a result of several lawsuits brought by the International Union of Electrical, Radio and Machine Workers (IUE), the pay rates of some jobs held mainly by women have been raised. A selection of the job titles compared in one case is shown in Table 15; similar jobs were matched and the issue in contention was their relative worth. As the table shows, the jobs were almost entirely segregated by sex, and the highest paid women's job was paid less than the lowest paid men's job. As a result of the settlement, these women's jobs were generally raised several grade levels, although only four of them were judged to be of fully equal worth to similar men's jobs. After the settlement, the union negotiated wage increases for many more jobs held by women, which were not as readily comparable to those held by men but were comparable to some of the women's jobs that had been raised.[8]

A different kind of evidence comes from a situation in which job evaluation procedures were used explicitly for the purpose of assessing the existence and extent of pay discrimination based on sex. In 1974 a study was conducted of state government jobs in the State of Washington (Willis, 1974, 1976). A claim had been made that the existing practice of pegging the pay rates of state employees to prevailing rates in the private sector was discriminatory because the private sector traditionally underpaid jobs held mainly by women. To assess this claim, the study compared the pay rates of jobs held mainly by women with the pay rates of jobs of "comparable worth" held mainly by men. A total of 121 positions, in which at least 70 percent of incumbents were of the same sex, were chosen for evaluation. The job evaluation plan used, which was developed by Norman Willis and Associates of Seattle, was substantially similar to the Hay Associates plan (see Treiman, 1979:21–23). Of the 121 positions, 59 were filled at least 70 percent by men and 62 were filled at least 70 percent by women. Figure 2 shows that in the State of Washington, jobs held mainly by women were paid substantially less than jobs of comparable value, as defined by the job evaluation formula, held mainly by men: the pay rates for the jobs held mainly by women averaged about 80 percent of the pay rates for jobs with the same number of job evaluation points held mainly by men.[9]

---

[8] Newman (1976:271) writes:

> The psychology here is interesting. "Jane," a grade 11, did not compare her job with "John's" grade 14 job; instead she compared herself with "Sandra," a grade 8 who was a plaintiff in the lawsuit, as a result of which "Sandra" also became a grade 11. "Jane" was sure she was worth three grades more than "Sandra"—but did not know she was worth as much as "John," who had been performing a "man's" job.

[9] For this study it is possible to apply Birnbaum's test (see Chapter 2, note 17) to confirm that the underpayment, relative to their worth, of jobs held by women is not a statistical artifact. For the 121 occupations included in Figure 2, let $X$ equal job worth points, $Y$ equal the average monthly salary, and $F$ equal 1 for the 62 jobs held mainly by women and 0 for the 59 jobs held mainly by men (computed from Willis, 1974). For these occupations $\beta_{YF.X}$ is $-.406$ and $\beta_{XF.Y}$ is $.832$. That is, it is true that (1) holding constant job worth, jobs held mainly by women are paid less than jobs held mainly by men (the estimated difference—the metric coefficient of $F$—is \$175 per month, a bit more than 20 percent of the average salary for all jobs) and that (2) holding constant salaries, jobs held mainly by women score higher in terms of job worth points than jobs held mainly by men. Using Birnbaum's criterion, discrimination is clearly present.

TABLE 15 Hourly Wage Rates Before and After the 1972 General Electric Settlement, Fort Wayne, Indiana

| Jobs Held Mainly by Women | | | Jobs Held Mainly by Men | |
| --- | --- | --- | --- | --- |
| Original Grade and Rate | Jobs Title (Percent Female) | New Grade and Rate[a] | Original Grade and Rate[a] | Job Title (Percent Female) |
| (7) $3.14 | Lead maker (100) | (9) $3.255 | (13) $3.55 | Artos lead maker (0) |
| (8) 3.20 | Janitress (100) | (13) 3.55 | (13) 3.55 | Janitor (13) |
| (9) 3.255 | Load coils (100) | (12) 3.465 | (13) 3.55 | Insulate coils (0) |
| (9) 3.255 | Stacking (89) | (12)[b] 3.465 | (14) 3.625 | Stacking (0) |
| (9) 3.255 | Compound pourer (100) | (12)[b] 3.465 | (15) 3.725 | Pourer (0) |
| (10) 3.305 | Coil winder (100) | (14) 3.625 | (14) 3.625 | Stator winder (0) |
| (10) 3.305 | Back gear winder (100) | (14) 3.625 | (16) 3.835 | Type 1 winding (25) |
| (10) 3.305 | Motor assembly (100) | (14) 3.625 | (16) 3.835 | Motor assembly (0) |
| (11) 3.385 | Surge test (100) | (15) 3.725 | (16) 3.865 | Surge test (12) |
| (12) 3.465 | Respooler (100) | (15) 3.725 | (15) 3.725 | Salvage (0) |
| (12) 3.465 | Repair stator (100) | (15) 3.725 | (16) 3.865 | Motor parts repair (0) |
| (12) 3.465 | Stator repair (100) | (15) 3.725 | (17) 4.005 | Motor repair (0) |
| (12) 3.465 | Receiving inspector (100) | (18) 4.20 | (18) 4.20 | Receiving inspector (0) |
| (12) 3.465 | Thermocouple test (100) | (14) 3.63 | (19) 4.40 | Plotter test (0) |

[a] Labor grades 14 and 16 have two different hourly wage rates. In each grade the higher of the two rates is the regular rate; the lower rate is an incentive rate, a minimum rate allows for additional incentive pay whenever performance in a job is above the standard set for the job.

[b] Some were raised to grade (14) at $3.625 per hour.

SOURCE: Adapted from Newman, 1976:270.

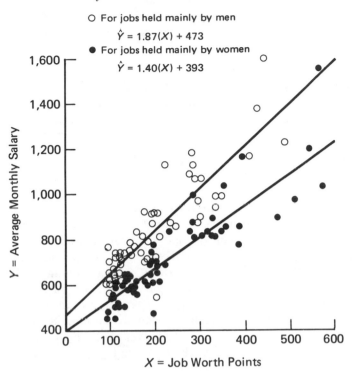

FIGURE 2   Scatterplot of monthly salaries by job worth points, for 59 jobs held mainly by men and 62 jobs held mainly by women in the Washington State public service.

SOURCE: Computed from Willis, 1974.

One of the features of wage differentials between jobs held by men and by women is that they become customary, accepted as the standard rates for the jobs. Evolving wage structures in a community come to reflect these differentials, which are passed between internal and external labor markets. Area wage surveys reproduce these differentials. If institutional factors such as those reviewed here do operate in the labor market, then relying solely on area wage rates to establish pay rates for a particular firm will incorporate those differentials into that firm's wage structure. Those differentials will be based on all factors, including productivity and discrimination, that create differentials in earnings between women and men in the wider market. By use of the "going wage" as a standard to set pay rates the wages of a (nondiscriminating) firm will be biased by the discrimination of other firms in the market. In the State of Washington case reviewed above, the cause of the "underpayment" of jobs held mainly by women was not a result of an overtly discriminatory act on the part of the employer but simple conformity to the prevailing pay rate of the private sector.

## DISCRIMINATION IN LABOR MARKETS

Although the institutional approach to understanding labor markets is not itself a theory of discrimination, it does view labor markets as inherently rigid and balkanized. The approach thus provides a basis for viewing discrimination as an integral part of both labor market processes and their outcomes. The labor market, incorporating a range of political, social, and economic forces, is seen to create an institutional context in which groups with different interests attempt to stabilize or enhance their positions. In this context discrimination can be understood to be one of the important mechanisms that have contributed historically to the creation of segmented labor markets. In addition, the ways work is organized and the associated patterns of productivity and wages—in both the secondary and the primary segments—incorporate and reproduce patterns of unequal access and disparate rewards for different groups of workers. Rigidities such as custom, tradition, barriers to mobility, and administrative rules tend to prevent change and to reinforce established patterns. Thus, hierarchy and inequality, including discrimination, are seen to be part of labor markets.

In the institutional view of labor markets, discrimination would be expected to take the form of segregation into different jobs rather than of lower pay for identical jobs (Blau and Jusenius, 1976; Blau, 1977; Stevenson, 1978). This is so because internal labor markets in large firms typically function with the aid of work rules that are bureaucratically enforced and uniformly applied and administered; because these rules specify that everyone in the same job category should be treated similarly; and because sex, race, and ethnic differences have recently come to be perceived as unfair (and indeed illegal, with the passage of the Equal Pay Act and the Civil Rights Act).

We must stress, however, that in an institutional framework neither the fact nor the form of discrimination is inevitable—in fact, important changes have occurred within the past two decades. Minorities and women in earlier times were subjected to discrimination of various forms: lower pay for doing work identical to that performed by non-minority men; *de jure* and customary exclusion from some jobs; inadequate education because of segregated (and unequal) schooling; and *de facto* exclusion from some jobs because of residential segregation. While none of these forms of discrimination is absent from contemporary

American society, their importance has been reduced by legal, social, and political intervention.

The institutional view of labor markets helps to explain how discrimination can occur and persist through job segregation that confines women and minorities to low-wage jobs. There are, of course, other views of how discrimination occurs within or through labor markets, although no economic theory attempts to explain the origins of discrimination. Some theorists rely on the concept of "tastes," people's preference for working with or hiring their own kind (Becker, 1971); others suggest economic advantage is the motive, either of white male workers (Bergmann, 1974; Madden, 1975) or of employers (Reich, 1978); still others suggest that discrimination occurs because it minimizes the cost to employers of doing business (Phelps, 1972). Most agree on the primacy of job segregation as the mechanism of discrimination. Moreover, since the persistence of discrimination over time cannot be explained by conventional models of the labor market (which posit perfect mobility, information, and access), most theories of discrimination incorporate departures from these assumptions in an attempt to better represent the actual behavior of labor markets.

In one of the earliest models of discrimination, Gary Becker (1957, 1971), incorporating a central element of neoclassical theory, relied on "tastes" of employers, employees, or customers as the motivating force behind discriminatory behavior. He suggests that people's tastes for discrimination can be satisfied or bought off at certain prices. For example, if whites do not want to work with blacks, they can be encouraged to do so only by being offered wages that are high enough to offset their distaste for working with blacks. If employers do not want to hire blacks, however, the employers can be encouraged to do so only by hiring blacks at wage rates low enough to compensate for their distaste. If consumers do not want to buy products made or served by blacks, they will buy them only if the prices are low enough to offset their distaste. Becker's hypothesis is that in such cases resources are being allocated inefficiently, and competitive market forces would be expected to eliminate the wage and price differentials over time.

In another influential model of discrimination, Barbara Bergmann (1971, 1974) applied the concept of overcrowding to race and sex discrimination. Her model is based on the assumption that the distaste for hiring minorities and women is so strong that employers exclude them from many jobs. This has the effect of increasing the supply of labor available to fill the jobs that are open to women and minorities, which in turn drives the market wage for these jobs down relative to what it would be if there were no restrictions on occupational opportunities.

Similarly, the wages of favored groups are higher than they would be otherwise because of their relative undersupply. Again, in this model resources are being inefficiently allocated; the free movement of workers would result in more total product. In postulating a bifurcated labor market Bergmann departs somewhat from the neoclassical concepts of perfect competition, mobility, and information, in that in her model men and women and blacks and whites are not able to compete with each other for jobs. Yet, just as in Becker's model, discrimination is expected to disappear over time because any employer who does not exclude minorities or women would have a competitive advantage over those who incur higher production costs by excluding them.

Phelps (1972) and others have developed the concept of statistical discrimination. This model, like Thurow's queuing model (1969, 1975) and early models of the dual labor market (Doeringer and Piore, 1971), postulates that to minimize training and turnover costs employers attempt to find the most productive workers for jobs requiring stability and long or costly training. If employers *believe that* women and minorities are less productive or have higher turnover rates, they will not hire them. They do not necessarily have tastes for discrimination; they are simply minimizing the costs of screening prospective employees by summarily eliminating those they think are likely to be unproductive or costly workers—generalizing about individuals on the basis of their perception of group characteristics. Whether or not these workers are less productive, they are barred from the opportunity to take "good" jobs. The model recognizes that employers do not have perfect information and that obtaining information incurs costs. The workers thus excluded take other jobs, for which turnover costs are perceived by employers to be less important. Or, if employers hire such workers for good jobs, it is at wage rates low enough to compensate employers for their expected higher costs. Of course, when employers' beliefs are so erroneous that the costs of screening would be more than compensated by the quality of the workers erroneously excluded, discrimination would be expected to abate or disappear over time, because employers who do not hold such erroneous beliefs would have a competitive advantage.

As Cain (1976) has noted, the human capital approach, the approach most commonly used in developing models to measure the extent of discrimination in the labor market, does not provide information about the possible mechanisms of discrimination. Such models attempt only to measure the results. As we note in Chapter 2, these studies indicate that women earn much lower returns on their human capital than do men, and that the earnings differential cannot be explained by sex differences in characteristics of workers thought to affect their productivity.

Despite the inability to measure precisely the various sources of wage differentials and the plethora of postulated mechanisms of discrimination, researchers agree that job segregation is an important source of the difference in wages between men and women. In our view, although the concentration of women in lower-paying jobs exists at least in part because of women's choices, it also results from the exclusionary practices of employers and from the systematic underpayment of jobs held mainly by women. Wages are higher in some jobs and lower in others than they would be in the absence of job segregation. In particular, the wage rates of jobs traditionally held by women are depressed relative to what they would be if women had equal opportunity in the labor market.

## CONCLUSION

The main conclusion of our analysis of labor markets is that observed market wages incorporate the effects of many institutional factors, including discrimination. This conclusion has three corollaries. First, market wages cannot be used as the sole standard for judging the relative worth of jobs. Second, in order to end discrimination, policy interventions to alter market outcomes may be required. Third, because of the complexity of market processes, actions intended to have one result may well turn out to have other, even perverse, consequences.

The first corollary requires no additional comment. With regard to the second, we simply note that over the years a variety of strategies designed to alter market outcomes have been proposed and implemented. These strategies include programs to encourage additional schooling and job training; programs to encourage the employment of the disadvantaged; improvements in job information and job search techniques; equal opportunity legislation designed to eliminate the discriminatory practices of employers, labor unions, and employment agencies; and programs to encourage women and minorities to train for and enter untraditional jobs. In addition, the coverage of the federally mandated minimum wage has been expanded over the years to protect workers in many of the lowest-paid jobs, such as those in domestic service, agriculture, laundries, restaurants and hotels, and fast food chains—jobs in which women and minorities are overrepresented. Historically, organization by both employees and employers and regulation by government agencies have been the methods most often used to attempt to alter market outcomes.

With respect to the third corollary, any policy of intervention requires that full consideration be given to the complexity of labor markets and to all the forces that influence market outcomes. Because so many factors are influential, policies to alter outcomes that focus only on selected factors may not have the intended effects. Equal employment opportunity programs, for example, focus on the demand side of the market by attempting to influence employer hiring, promotion, and compensation policies. But if only some employers are affected by the regulations, those with government contracts, for example, they may hire minorities or women away from employers without government contracts, and the net effect may be that the employment of minorities or women has not increased as much as was expected (for an example in construction see Flanagan, 1976). Similarly, if government efforts succeed either in raising the wages paid to minorities and women above the levels employers think are warranted or in placing minorities and women in jobs that employers think are inappropriate for them, employers may substitute other factors of production. Other changes in the economic environment faced by the employer may also occur simultaneously with affirmative action efforts and may have countervailing effects. For example, one study claims that since the well-publicized consent decree involving American Telephone and Telegraph, the rate at which technological change has displaced women workers appears to have increased more rapidly than previously predicted by the company (Hacker, 1978).

Strategies that focus on the supply side of the market are similarly limited if they are not implemented in connection with complementary strategies. Women and minority workers can be trained in new fields, for example, but if employers refuse to hire them, market outcomes will not be altered. Strategies that focus on improving the operation of labor markets—by increasing the information available about jobs, for example—assume that both demand and supply are adequate so that once workers and employers find out about each other they can come to mutually beneficial terms. It must also be recognized that in our economy not everyone can have a "good," high-paying job. Our economy generates low-wage jobs as well as high-wage jobs; attempts to prevent their being filled in this country may simply result in the exportation of low-wage jobs. The complexity of the labor market does not mean, of course, that market outcomes cannot be altered. It does mean that no single type of policy is likely to be effective by itself and that any strategy to alter outcomes in one part of the labor market must take into account the likely consequences in other parts as well as the structure of the economy itself.

The committee is convinced by the evidence, taken together, that women are systematically underpaid. Policies designed to promote equal access to all employment opportunities will affect the underpayment of women workers only slowly. Equal access to employment opportunities may be expected to be more effective for new entrants than for established workers and more effective for those who have invested less in skills than for those who have invested more. Since many women currently in the labor force have invested years of training time in their particular skills (e.g., nursing, teaching, librarianship, and secretarial work), access to other jobs (e.g., physicianship, plumbing, engineering, or sales) may not be preferred. For these reasons the committee believes that the strategy of "comparable worth," that is, equal pay for jobs of equal worth, merits consideration as an alternative policy of intervention in the pay-setting process wherever women are systematically underpaid.

The viability of a strategy of paying jobs in accordance with their "worth" requires, first, that an appropriate mechanism, other than current market wage rates, can be found to measure the relative worth of jobs to an employer and, second, that wages commensurate with worth can be set and paid by the employer. In cases in which wage costs, productivity, profitability, conditions in product markets, or economic growth permits the new costs to be absorbed, this strategy provides a direct method of redress for wage discrimination due to occupational segregation. Since much of the wage differential arises because women work in low-wage firms and men work in high-wage firms, however, even a comparable worth approach, applied to single firms, would not entirely eliminate the differential. For this reason and because, given the complexity of labor markets, a comparable worth strategy may have unanticipated and unintended effects, it cannot be viewed as a panacea. Raising the wages of jobs held by women through a comparable worth strategy might have various effects. On one hand, employers might alter the nature of the jobs women hold in order to encourage longer job tenures and lower turnover rates, thereby reducing costs and making their investments in women pay off. Higher wages might also encourage employers to offer women more on-the-job training and skill enhancement programs. On the other hand, a comparable worth strategy might reduce employment either because employers shift to alternative, less labor-intensive methods of production or (if the new labor costs were paid and passed on) because consumers might switch to other, less expensive goods or services.[10] We want to point out, however, that the

---

[10] Gregory and Duncan (1981) investigated the relevance of labor market segmentation theory to Australia's recent efforts to increase the wages of occupations filled mainly by women. They suggest that the wage increases did not negatively affect the number of women employed, in part because many employers of women were sufficiently insulated from competitive market forces to absorb the higher costs.

strategy of comparable worth is conceptually similar to earlier policies of directly altering wages by raising them above previous market rates, such as the minimum wage and overtime premium provisions of the Fair Labor Standards Act and the Equal Pay Act of 1963. Employers were certainly able to hire the workers they needed at rates lower than those prescribed by the new provisions; they were, however, required by law to pay more. Economists are still debating the merit of these provisions and attempting to identify and measure their effects on the amount and terms of employment (Levitan and Belous, 1979).

While further study of the possible effects of a comparable worth strategy is certainly required, the committee believes that policies devised to alter pay structures so that jobs are rewarded in a nondiscriminatory manner—that is, commensurate with their demands and requirements rather than in ways based on the sex, race, or ethnicity of those who hold them—are clearly desirable. It is not, however, an easy task to ascertain for any particular job whether its pay rate includes discriminatory elements. Chapter 4 discusses the potential usefulness of various proposed procedures for identifying and eliminating discriminatory elements of pay differences among jobs within an individual firm.

# 4 Wage-Adjustment Approaches to Overcoming Discrimination

## INTRODUCTION

We have presented evidence indicating that men and women tend to be employed at different jobs and that jobs held mainly by women tend to pay less than jobs held mainly by men, even when account is taken of differences in the complexity and difficulty of jobs and the qualifications and experience of incumbents. Insofar as such pay differences result from the concentration of men and women in different firms, the issue is not one of pay equity but one of equality of access to firms. When women are concentrated disproportionately in the low-paying jobs within a firm, however, the question arises: can differences in the average pay of men and women be accounted for entirely by differences in their access to or preference for high-paying and low-paying jobs, or are the pay rates influenced by the sex composition of jobs? In the latter case the remedy would be to adjust the pay rates of jobs so as to remove what would be considered the discriminatory component. Such a procedure requires, however, the development of a means for identifying whether and what portion of pay differences in jobs within a firm are discriminatory.

One approach to unraveling the components of pay differentials is to measure the worth of jobs directly, using any of a number of job evaluation procedures. The concept of comparable worth is that jobs of equal worth should be paid equally. The demand and supply of particular skills and similar factors are regarded as legitimate bases of pay differences among jobs only insofar as such factors are explicitly included in the formulas for specifying job worth.[1] In this approach, instances of possible discrimination in pay are identified by using the job worth hierarchy resulting from application of the job evaluation plan as a standard against which to assess actual pay rates.

Acceptance of a comparable worth approach—the attempt to measure the worth of jobs directly on the basis of their content—does not require an absolute standard by which the value or worth of *all* jobs can be measured. In the judgment of the committee, no such standard exists nor, in our society, is likely to exist. The relative worth of jobs reflects value judgments as to what features of jobs ought to be compensated, and such judgments typically vary from industry to industry, even from firm to firm. Paying jobs according to their worth requires only that whatever characteristics of jobs are regarded as worthy of compensation by an employer should be equally so regarded irrespective of the sex, race, or ethnicity of job incumbents.

The use of job evaluation procedures without modification may not always be appropriate, however, because some job evaluation plans are designed in such a way that they reproduce whatever biases exist in the pay practices current when the plans were introduced. Moreover, not all employers who use job evaluation plans base pay rates solely on the job worth hierarchy implied by the job evaluation plan in use; in such cases inferences regarding possible discrimination must rest not on specific instances of underpayment of jobs relative to their "worth" but on a pattern of underpayment for jobs held mainly by women or minorities. To cope with these complications, we explore two modifications to the conventional job evaluation approach: a multiple regression approach that includes "percent female" among the variables used to predict pay rates, and the use of pay rates of white men in jobs held mainly by white men as a standard of equitable pay. These approaches have potential value in developing bias-free job evaluation plans and in identifying instances of discrimination in pay.

In this chapter we first review the conventional job evaluation approach and the two modifications, commenting on their strengths and weaknesses. We then demonstrate the use of these procedures to correct discriminatory pay rates. Throughout we suggest a number of areas in which additional research is necessary before definitive conclusions can be reached or unqualified recommendations offered regarding the desirability of adopting any of the procedures reviewed.

---

[1] For example, particular skills may be in demand because of the newness of a technology; if so, a job factor indicating the newness of technology for each job could be added to the job evaluation plan used (see Remick, 1978).

# CONVENTIONAL JOB EVALUATION APPROACHES TO ASSESSING PAY RATES

## METHODS OF JOB EVALUATION

At the present time in the United States many large private companies, the federal government, and many state governments make use of some form of formal job evaluation as an aid to establishing pay rates for jobs. Although job evaluation systems differ in details of design and implementation, almost all conform to a common methodology and underlying logic: all the jobs in the unit being analyzed (firms, division, or other)[2] are described; the descriptions are then rated or evaluated according to one or more "compensable factors" (features defined as legitimate bases for pay differentials); the ratings are added in some way to create a total score, sometimes called a job worth score; and the scores are used—sometimes alone and sometimes with other information—to assign the jobs to pay classes.[3]

Particularly in large firms with large internal labor markets, it is not always evident how to set pay rates for different jobs. Even when a firm is committed to paying the going rate in the local labor market for each job, such information is not always available, and, as we note in Chapter 3, many jobs are filled entirely from within a firm, so that there is no going rate to apply. Moreover, a large firm may be the only or the largest employer in town and hence be in the position of defining the going rate for many jobs. In these contexts, job evaluation systems prove useful as a way of setting pay rates.

One type of job evaluation plan, known generically as the point method or factor point method, is used in many organizations and is therefore used to illustrate this discussion. In this type of job evaluation plan a set of compensable factors is chosen. For each factor a scale is devised representing increasing levels of "worth," and each level is assigned a given number of points. Each job is rated on each factor separately, then assigned the corresponding number of points for the rated level on each factor. The points are totaled to yield the job worth score.

---

[2] "Other" may be an entire industry; a job evaluation plan for production jobs in the steel industry is such an example. While for convenience our discussion usually refers to "firms," it should be understood as applicable to all compensation systems, however they may be organized.

[3] The properties of existing job evaluation plans are described in more detail in the committee's interim report to the Equal Employment Opportunity Commission (Treiman, 1979).

Many of the factor point job evaluation systems in use today were developed by using a firm's existing pay structure to statistically determine which attributes of jobs best predict their pay rates. In this approach a set of factors that is thought likely to be related to existing pay differences among jobs is identified—factors representing differences in skill, effort, responsibility, and working conditions. Each job is scored on each of the factors. These factors are then used to predict existing pay rates (usually via the statistical technique of multiple regression analysis), and those factors contributing substantially to the prediction are included in the job evaluation plan, with weights proportional to their contribution. The factors and factor weights can then be used to assign pay rates for new jobs and to adjust the pay rates of existing jobs that are overpaid or underpaid relative to the predictions of the formula. This method provides an empirically derived underlying structure with which the pay rates of all jobs in a firm can be brought into conformity. This is sometimes called a "policy-capturing" approach—the implicit policy underlying the existing pay system is made explicit. Job evaluation plans developed in this way necessarily produce hierarchies of job worth that are closely related to existing pay hierarchies: that is what they are designed to do.

Another way to develop a factor point job evaluation system is to define *a priori* a set of factors and factor weights that expresses what the employer believes are legitimate bases of pay differentials.[4] In both methods of developing factor point systems, job worth is defined by the factors that measure it, and jobs are assumed to deserve equal pay if they have equal total scores on the job worth scale.

In both of these methods, completely different kinds of jobs may have equal total job worth scores and hence be regarded as deserving equal pay. In a set of jobs with equal total scores, one job, for example, may entail great responsibility, while another job may require great skill. The major purpose of job evaluation systems, however designed, is to make the content of different kinds of jobs commensurable for the purpose of determining pay rates. While this is difficult to do, and we discuss a number of the difficulties below, we do not believe it is impossible in principle. In our discussion of job evaluation we accept the criteria of worth implicit in each plan—"worth" being determined by those features of jobs that are identified and measured—and focus on

---

[4] "Employer" as used here refers to whoever sets policy for a firm, regardless of how policy decisions are made. Decisions regarding compensation and job evaluation plans may well be the outgrowth of union-management negotiations or the work of committees that include members drawn from all levels within a firm.

ways to improve the measurement of jobs according to these criteria. Although we considered the potential use of other criteria—for example, productivity—we felt it would be most useful to concentrate on the criteria that are currently used.[5]

Because formal job evaluation plans purport to measure the worth of jobs—in the precise sense of measuring the factors that are regarded by employers as legitimate bases of pay differentials among jobs—it has been suggested that such plans can be used to arrive at objectively fair pay rates for jobs and thus to resolve charges of pay discrimination based on sex, race, or ethnicity. Specifically, actual pay rates could be compared with the pay rates that would prevail if jobs were paid according to their job worth scores, and the difference taken as a measure of possible discrimination. Furthermore, if the difference between actual and predicted pay rates were shown to be correlated with the sex, race, or ethnic composition of occupational categories, then a strong suspicion would be created that pay practices are discriminatory, and appropriate action could be taken. That is, if the jobs with actual wage rates lower than indicated by the job worth scores tended to be held disproportionately by women or minorities, and if the jobs with actual wage rates higher than indicated by the job worth scores tended to be held by men or by nonminorities, then the existence of discriminatory pay practices would be implied.

In the judgment of the committee, four aspects of formal job evaluation procedures are important in assessing their practical application in developing pay plans and in resolving complaints of pay discrimination, particularly in a labor force highly segregated by sex, race, and ethnicity. (The first three of these features are reviewed in greater detail in the committee's interim report; see Treiman, 1979.) First, the ranking

---

[5] The committee also concluded that with rare exceptions the difficulties of measuring productivity are very great. To be useful in job evaluation the relative average productivity (the contribution to output) of each job would have to be measured. For example, to assess the productivity of hospital workers the relative contribution of nurses, doctors, orderlies, secretaries, and maintenance workers to hospital output would have to be determined. At the present time, however, there is no agreement on how to measure hospital output, and little attempt has been made to assess the relative contributions of various hospital workers (Scott, 1979). While an employer may want to include productivity measures in job evaluation plans when they become available, the factors currently identified in job evaluation plans reflect employers' conceptions of what should be remunerated. For example, some plans emphasize skill more than responsibility; some do the opposite. Presumably these differences reflect, at least in part, employers' judgments about what enhances the performance of their firms. Further research on the measurement of the productivity of jobs and research on the incorporation of productivity measures in job evaluation plans are advisable.

of jobs tends to be highly dependent on which factors are used in the evaluation and how heavily each factor is weighted. And as we have already noted, the principal method for deriving factor weights in most currently used job evaluation plans pegs them to current pay rates, therby reflecting existing pay differences between men and women (and between minority and nonminority) workers. Second, like other methods of establishing pay rates, job evaluation involves judgments, making it possible for well-known processes of stereotyping to result in an undervaluation of jobs held mainly by women. Third, many employers use more than one job evaluation plan in their firms (e.g., one for shop jobs and one for office jobs), a policy that makes it difficult to compare the worth of jobs—or to determine the likelihood of discrimination in pay— among different sectors of a firm. Fourth, the interpretation of the differences between actual and predicted pay rates as evidence of discrimination requires strong assumptions regarding the adequacy of the prediction model and the measurement of the variables included in the model—assumptions that may be difficult to satisfy in practice. Each of these features is discussed below.

### FACTORS AND FACTOR WEIGHTS

Although in principle a very large set of compensable factors could be developed, in practice most job evaluation systems use a similar small set of factors. This is due in part to the propensity of designers of job evaluation systems to borrow factors from previously developed systems with only minor modifications. In addition, the choice of factors no doubt reflects the industrial origin of job evaluation plans. Their use was initially in factories, and the job characteristics chosen for evaluation tended to emphasize shop knowledge, responsibility for equipment, strength requirements, work hazards, and so on. Job evaluation plans have subsequently been designed specifically for the evaluation of office jobs as well as executive jobs. It is probably true, however, that the job evaluation systems currently available do not correspond very closely to the character of the contemporary labor force, which is increasingly concentrated in technical and service jobs that did not exist when most plans were developed (for example, jobs involving automated information processing, such as computer operator, data entry clerk, airline reservations agent, etc.). It is not clear how important this issue is, but a question must be raised as to how well these new jobs are dealt with by systems designed to evaluate quite different sorts of jobs. Since such technical and service jobs are often held by women, any inadequacy in the ability of existing job evaluation plans to measure properly their compensable features may undercut the usefulness of these plans in resolving pay discrimination disputes. In our judgment, consideration should be given to redesigning job evaluation systems currently in use to take account of changes in the content of jobs in the American economy in the 40 years since most of them were initially developed.

Despite the fact that most job evaluation plans appear to tap the same basic features of jobs—skill, effort, responsibility, and working conditions—the particular operational indicators of the factors may vary more widely, a possibility with important consequences. For example, "skill" is sometimes measured operationally by the amount of experience required to become fully trained in a job and sometimes by the amount of formal education required to qualify for a job. Clerical jobs, for example, tend to entail considerable formal education but little actual on-the-job training, while the reverse tends to be true of craft jobs. The choice of which operational indicator of skill is used in a job evaluation system could have substantial impact on the job worth scores of these two categories of jobs. Furthermore, since clerical jobs tend to be held mainly by women and craft jobs to be held mainly by men, the choice of indicators could effectively determine the outcome of any analysis of whether pay differences between these job categories involve discrimination on the basis of sex. Proper use of job evaluation techniques to resolve disputes involving pay discrimination depends on clear understanding of precisely what factors are used in the evaluation formula.

The relative weight accorded the different compensable factors used in a job evaluation plan can have substantial impact on the resulting hierarchy of job worth. That is, different weightings of factors can substantially alter the ordering of jobs. If the content of the jobs held by men and women or by minorities and nonminorities differs substantially, then different weightings of the factors can result in different outcomes as to the average worth of jobs held by men and women or by minorities and nonminorities, and hence in different judgments regarding the presence or extent of pay discrimination on the basis of sex or minority status. (For a more detailed discussion of this point see Treiman, 1979:53–54.)

We noted above that a frequently used method of determining the relative weight to be accorded each factor in developing a job evaluation plan is to predict existing market wage rates from a set of potential job evaluation factors. This method, although it has advantages, has two major drawbacks.

One of these drawbacks is technical. The resulting weights may vary substantially, depending on the set of jobs chosen for the prediction and the data base used in determining the average wages of those jobs.[6] In the typical application a subset of all jobs in a firm is used to determine factor weights: these are often called "key" or "benchmark" jobs. If, for example, only the highest-paid blue-collar jobs and the lowest-paid white-collar jobs in a firm are used as benchmark jobs and blue-collar and white-collar jobs typically have different characteristics, then the weights for the white-collar job characteristics derived by this procedure would be unusually low and those for the blue-collar job characteristics unusually high, compared with their actual compensation in the firm. Hence the choice of benchmark jobs can affect the weights derived. Second, even if the benchmark jobs are themselves representative of all jobs in a firm, a wide range of wage rates typically exists for each job, and the choice of wage used to represent the job (minimum, mid-point, mean, etc.) can affect the weights resulting from the procedure. These technical difficulties mean that the derived weights may not adequately reflect compensation. This aspect of the implementation of job evaluation procedures is an extremely important one, and care must be taken that even a well-designed system is not poorly implemented at this stage.

The second major drawback of using existing wages to derive factor weights is that the weights will then necessarily reflect in turn any biases that exist in market wages. To the extent that existing wages incorporate the effects of discriminatory practices (and we argue in Chapter 3 that those effects can be substantial in some cases), the weights derived from those wages as well as the resulting job worth scores also incorporate those effects. It is hardly optimal to use job evaluation scores as a standard against which to assess the legitimacy of existing pay differences among jobs if the job evaluation scores themselves are designed to replicate as closely as possible existing pay differences.

On the other hand, using existing wages to derive factor weights has the advantage, from the point of view of the employer and many em-

---

[6] In a typical prediction exercise, a set of jobs has average wage rates $Y$ and preliminary, arbitrarily specified scores on job worth factors $J_i$ $(i = 1, \ldots, n)$. An equation of the following type is estimated,

$$\hat{Y} = a + \sum_{i=1}^{n} b_i J_i ,$$

where $Y$ represents the estimated wage rates of the jobs, and $b_i$ represent the estimated weights for the factors $J_i$. The constant term, $a$, and the weights, $b_i$, are derived, using multiple regression techniques, such that the "residuals," $Y - \hat{Y}$, are as small as possible (specifically, $\Sigma(Y - \hat{Y})^2$ is minimized for the sample). The weights can then be used to rescale the factors for use in deriving job worth scores.

ployees, of by and large preserving customary wage relationships among jobs and of formalizing an evaluation of the relative worth of different attributes of jobs that already exists implicitly. The rationalization of a system already largely in place is likely to be far less disruptive than imposition of a substantially different hierarchy and criteria of job worth. Moreover, when—as is sometimes done—area wage rates rather than a firm's own wage rates are used, employers can be reasonably certain that their internal pay structure is consonant with external market rewards and that their pay scale will enable them to recruit and retain the necessary workers.

## THE ROLE OF JUDGMENT

It is important to recognize that job evaluation ultimately rests on judgments. Jobs are described in terms of their tasks, duties, and responsibilities, and these descriptions are rated or ranked with respect to some set of factors. The factor ratings are seldom based on objective information; rather, they represent judgments about such amorphous features of jobs as the responsibility entailed or the experience required. The nature of job evaluation makes it possible for bias to enter at two points: in the writing of the job descriptions and in the evaluation of the descriptions with respect to a set of factors.

One can question to what extent traditional stereotypes regarding the complexity and responsibility of different types of work are reflected in job descriptions. Unfortunately, there is no evidence on this issue: to our knowledge there have been no studies of the accuracy or validity of job descriptions. Such studies would be extremely useful. Moreover, methods of systematic job analysis, such as structured job analysis and task analysis, ought to be explored for their applicability to job evaluation—in particular, the job component method of job evaluation (McCormick and Ilgen, 1980:Ch. 18), which uses structured job analysis.

One can also question to what extent sex stereotypes may affect the evaluation process. That is, are jobs held by women evaluated differently from jobs held by men, even when their content is virtually identical? The evidence in answer to this question is very sparse. Almost no evidence is available that pertains directly to sex stereotyping in the evaluation of *jobs*; there is, however, very strong evidence that female *workers* are evaluated as less worthy than male workers with identical characteristics. This evidence derives from a genre of studies in experimental social psychology in which subjects are presented with a set of vignettes describing the performance or qualifications of individuals and asked to rate them on one or several dimensions. Various aspects of the vignettes are systematically varied, and the effect of the variation on the ratings is studied. For our purposes, the variable of interest is the sex of the individual described in the vignette.

These studies are reviewed in detail in our interim report (Treiman, 1979:43–45). Here we report our conclusion (p. 45):

In a variety of contexts the mere fact of identifying a performance as done by a woman results in a lower evaluation and a lower likelihood of reward—hiring, promotion, etc.—than when the identical performance is attributed to a man. The only exception is when the performer is certified as competent on independent grounds; in such cases there is no significant tendency to evaluate women more poorly than men.

While most of the studies cited . . . refer to the evaluation of people rather than jobs, the evidence for sex stereotyping in job-related contexts is certainly strong enough to suggest the likelihood that sex stereotyping will pervade the evaluation of jobs strongly identified with one sex or the other. That is, it is likely that predominantly female jobs will be undervalued relative to predominantly male jobs in the same way that women are undervalued relative to men.

Given the paucity of the evidence, much additional work needs to be done to clarify to what extent and under what circumstances sex stereotyping is likely to be operating in the evaluation of jobs. For example, experimental studies of the same type as those cited above, in which job descriptions rather than job incumbents are evaluated, would be very useful. If the same description received a higher rating when identified with a "male" title than with a "female" title (e.g., waiter versus waitress, orderly versus nurse's aide), the process of sex stereotyping in the job evaluation process could be inferred. Moreover, ways should be explored to minimize the impact of stereotyped perceptions of jobs. One possibility would be to carry out job evaluations on the basis of job descriptions only, omitting job titles from the description.

MULTIPLE JOB EVALUATION PLANS IN A SINGLE FIRM

Another source of difficulty in using job evaluation plans to assess complaints of pay discrimination is the tendency of firms to use different job evaluation plans for different categories of workers. When more than one plan is used to evaluate the jobs in a firm, there is no way of directly comparing all jobs in that firm (unless a formula exists for translating the scores from one plan into the scores of the others, which is rarely the case). Since the job categories covered by different plans (typically shop, office, and executive jobs) tend to be highly segregated by sex, race, and ethnicity (i.e., women are overrepresented in office jobs and underrepresented in both shop and executive jobs; minorities are underrepresented in executive jobs), the use of job evaluation ratings to assess the existence of pay discrimination would appear to require the ability to make comparisons among as well as within the different plans.

The development of different job evaluation plans for different types of jobs appears to have two explanations: first, plans were originally developed for blue-collar jobs and only later for white-collar office and professional and executive jobs; second, different types of jobs are widely believed to have very different job characteristics. For example, manual dexterity, a factor thought to be important for most blue-collar jobs and some office jobs, is normally not thought to be important for professional and executive jobs. However, it is quite possible that, as the economy has changed, so has the nature of jobs. As both clerical and factory jobs are becoming more automated, they perhaps are coming to require skills that are more similar than they were previously. It has been suggested that job evaluation plans for technical jobs, which currently form a kind of bridge between plans for shop jobs and office jobs, could be used to evaluate all jobs. Moreover, some large firms and some state governments do in fact use a single plan for all workers, and the U.S. Department of Labor, in its *Dictionary of Occupational Titles*, describes all occupations in the economy using one set of factors.

The committee is divided on the question of whether the jobs usually found within a single firm can be adequately evaluated by a single job evaluation plan or whether several plans would be required to measure job characteristics adequately. Two issues are involved. First, should a given score on a given factor be worth the same amount for all jobs in a firm? Many on the committee would say yes—that is the meaning of comparable worth. If, for example, degree of responsibility differentiates supervisory from line jobs on the plant floor, it should do so in the office as well. Quite possibly, of course, an entire group of jobs could have the same rating on a particular factor. For example, a factor for undesirable working conditions might be scaled in such a way that all office jobs but only some plant jobs are scored in the lowest category, so in effect the factor would be relevant only in differentiating among plant jobs; this would not vitiate the applicability of a single job evaluation plan to an entire firm. The second, more difficult problem is whether indicators can be devised to measure accurately a given factor for all jobs in a firm. Is it possible, for example, to specify the meaning of responsibility in such a way as to differentiate between managerial jobs of greater and lesser responsibility and also to differentiate between shop jobs of greater and lesser responsibility? The answer to this question is uncertain. Not enough is yet known about the measurement of job characteristics to be able to assess the validity of job evaluation plans for different categories of jobs. More research on the nature of job characteristics and on the properties of job evaluation plans used throughout a firm is needed before the usefulness of such plans can be established.

MODELING AND MEASUREMENT

Two bases for specifying factors and factor weights in job evaluation formulas are reviewed above: (1) an *a priori* approach, in which the choice of compensable factors and their relative weights are decided as a matter of policy, without regard for existing pay practices, and (2) a policy-capturing approach, in which existing pay rates are predicted from a set of compensable factors via multiple regression procedures and weights are derived from the regression model. In the latter case, the adequacy of the predicted scores as the basis for assigning jobs to pay grades or for assessing whether jobs are "underpaid" or "overpaid" depends on the adequacy of the statistical model used to predict existing pay rates. There are a number of potential difficulties involved in regression procedures of this kind. First, if variables that in fact affect pay rates are omitted from the model, two distortions result: the predictions will be less accurate than otherwise and may be biased, and the relative weights of the variables included in the model will be distorted. Second, if variables in the model are measured imperfectly, they will appear to have less importance than they truly have. Third, if the functional form of the model is not correct, the predictions will be less accurate as well as distorted. There are now well-developed procedures for estimating regression models with nonlinearities and interactions of various kinds and for testing the relative adequacy of alternative functional forms, but these do not seem to have been widely used in job evaluation systems.

Techniques used in job evaluation have not kept pace with developments in econometrics, psychometrics, and sociological measurement. Serious attention should be given to the selection and measurement of compensable factors, the functional form of regression models, and assumptions about error structures, each of which can seriously affect the factor weights and the pay rates predicted by these models. Regression-based models of the type discussed here require considerable sensitivity and ingenuity on the part of the analyst; mechanical applications of the technique can easily produce seriously misleading results.

SUMMARY

A number of features of existing job evaluation systems make them less than optimal for use in the resolution of pay discrimination disputes. First, formal job evaluation systems order jobs by reference to a set of compensable factors—that is, factors thought to be legitimate bases of pay differentials. As we have shown, the factors and their relative weights are often chosen in such a way as to closely replicate existing wage hierarchies. For that reason, they can hardly serve as an independent standard against which to assess the possibility of bias in existing pay rates. Second, it is possible that the process of describing and evaluating jobs reflects pervasive cultural stereotypes regarding the relative worth of work traditionally done by men and work traditionally done by women. These features of job evaluation systems make it probable that their use as a standard of job worth understates the extent of differences in pay based on sex and perhaps on race or ethnicity. Third, most firms currently use more than one job evaluation plan, a practice that restricts comparisons between jobs to those within sectors of a firm—e.g., shop jobs, office jobs, or executive jobs. Finally, there are potentially serious technical shortcomings in the way regression procedures are used to create job evaluation formulas.

Nonetheless, it would be unwise to reject the use of job evaluation plans altogether. Despite their limitations, they do provide a systematic method of comparing jobs to determine whether they are fairly compensated. Because job evaluation plans as currently implemented are likely to understate the extent of differences in pay based on the sex, race, or ethnic composition of occupational categories, estimates of discrimination derived from the application of current job evaluation plans are probably low. Still, using job evaluation scores to determine pay rates will generally go some way toward reducing discriminatory differences in pay when they exist.

It may be possible to improve job evaluation plans. The committee urges job evaluation practitioners and users to scrutinize existing plans for fairness in light of the considerations reviewed here and in its interim report (Treiman, 1979). In addition, we urge further research into the many unresolved technical issues regarding job evaluation principles and practices. The techniques used in job evaluation plans have been for the most part designed and implemented by practitioners who have not been well grounded in advances in measurement in the social sciences. These procedures have not to date been subject to the kind of rigorous analytic scrutiny necessary to put them on a technically sound footing. Considering their potential usefulness in resolving wage discrimination disputes and the growing interest in that use, further research on techniques of job evaluation would be very valuable.

## STATISTICAL APPROACHES TO ASSESSING PAY RATES

The comparable worth approach attempts to use job evaluation procedures to determine "fair" rates of pay for jobs, but as we note above, that approach involves the difficulties inherent in using the job evaluation plans that are currently available. One of the main difficulties is that the factor weights used in job evaluation systems frequently are derived from a regression procedure designed to make job worth scores replicate existing wage hierarchies as closely as possible. When this is the case, the job worth scores themselves may reflect any existing bias.

The committee therefore explored two modifications of the statistical approach conventionally used in developing job evaluation plans. These procedues may be used both to modify existing job evaluation plans to reduce bias and to develop new bias-free job evaluation plans. They may also prove helpful in identifying specific instances of pay discrimination. The first is a multiple regression approach that, although analogous to the standard job evaluation procedure of using existing wages to derive factor weights, includes "percent female" among the predictor variables. The second is the use of wage rates of jobs held mainly by white men as a standard of "fair" wages. These are not, of course, the only statistical approaches available; indeed, we encourage the development and testing of alternative statistical approaches.

We wish to make clear at the outset that we discuss these approaches because of their potential and not because of their proven value. They are at present completely untried, and their application would entail the solution of many theoretical and practical problems of measurement. There is also a serious question as to whether the quality of the data generated by job evaluation plans in current use is adequate to sustain the kinds of statistical adjustments we describe. (The discussion in the previous section details some of the problems.) Moreover, there is considerable debate regarding the interpretation of the statistics generated by these adjustments (specifically, regression coefficients), especially given imperfect measurement (see Birnbaum, 1979). In order to encourage the kind of practical research and development that should be carried out in order to create technically sound procedures for identifying and correcting pay discrimination, we present these approaches as examples of two that might be considered.

INCLUDING "PERCENT FEMALE" IN THE ESTIMATION OF PAY
RATES

As we discuss above, the fact that men tend on the average to be paid more than women guarantees that any job evaluation factor that is correlated with the sex composition of jobs will receive some weight, and those factors that are more strongly correlated with sex composition will on the whole receive greater weight. Thus, the use of job evaluation plans perpetuates existing pay differences among jobs, which—as we have argued in Chapter 3—may reflect discriminatory as well as legitimate components of pay.

One potential method of removing the bias built into factor weights derived in the conventional way is to estimate the factor weights from an expanded equation that includes measures of the sex (or race or ethnic) composition of occupational categories. As we showed above (see note 6), the conventional approach to deriving factor weights for job evaluation plans is to estimate a regression equation of the form

$$\hat{Y} = a + \Sigma b_i J_i \qquad (1)$$

over a set of occupations in a firm, where $Y$ is the average pay rate of each occupation, the $J_i$ are potential compensable features of jobs (measures of skill, effort, responsibility, working conditions, etc.), and the $b_i$ are the estimated weights for the factors $J_i$.[7] Now consider a modification of eq. 1 of the form

$$\hat{Y} = a' + \Sigma b_i' J_i + cF, \qquad (2)$$

---

[7] While these equations are in linear form, as required by the regression estimating procedure, it is possible to represent quite complex relations, including interactions and nonlinearities of various kinds, by appropriate transformations of the variables. For example, an exponential equation of the form

$$Y = e^{a + \Sigma b_i X_i}$$

can be written in a mathematically equivalent way as a linear additive equation

$$\ln(Y) = a + \Sigma b_i X_i .$$

Similarly, an equation of the form

$$Y = a + b_1 X_1 + b_2 X_2 + b_3 X_1 X_2$$

can be rewritten as

$$Y = a + b_1 X_1 + b_2 X_2 + b_3 X_3$$

simply by defining $X_3 = X_1 X_2$. See Goldberger (1968), Mosteller and Tukey (1977), and Stolzenberg (1979) for a discussion of these and similar transformations.

where $Y$ and the $J_i$ are as before, $F$ is the percentage of incumbents of each job who are women, the $b_i{}'$ are the estimated weights for the factor $J_i$ (in general, these will not be the same as the corresponding coefficients, $b_i$, estimated by eq. 1), and $c$ is the weight for the percent female.

The coefficients, $b_i{}'$, associated with each of the compensable factors, $J_i$, can be interpreted as indicating the contribution of each factor in determining the average pay rate of workers in these occupations, holding constant each other factor, plus percent female. Specifically, each $b_i{}'$ indicates the number of dollars a one-point change in the factor score is worth, on the average, for occupations that have identical scores on the other factors and the same percent female. For example, suppose the first factor, $J_1$, indicates the number of months of training necessary to become fully qualified. Estimating the equation yields a value for the coefficient $b_1{}'$ that indicates how many dollars each month of training is worth. That is, for 2 jobs equal in all other respects except that one requires 2 months of training and the other requires 12 months of training, a difference in their average pay rates of $10b_1{}'$ dollars would be predicted, since they differ by 10 units on the variable $J_1$.

These coefficients differ from the corresponding coefficients in eq. 1, the conventional job evaluation equation, in that they are adjusted for the propensity of characteristics that distinguish between jobs held mainly by women and jobs held mainly by men to be heavily weighted as a consequence of the strong negative association in most firms between the percent female and the average earnings of jobs; the explicit inclusion of percent female in the equation is what adjusts the weights. Given the usual association between sex composition and earnings, job evaluation scales built by weighting the factors in proportion to the coefficients $b_i{}'$ from eq. 2 will ordinarily be less sex-biased than scales built by weighting the factors in proportion to the corresponding coefficients of eq. 1.

The coefficient $c$ indicates the effect of sex composition on pay rates for occupations that are identical with respect to all of the other variables. Specifically, $c$ indicates the difference in pay rates that would be expected on the average between two occupations that differ by one percentage point in their sex composition but are identical with respect to all other measured variables. As such, $c$ can be taken as a direct measure of potential discrimination. Whenever $c$ is significantly different from zero, the sex composition of occupations would have to be interpreted as a compensable factor—but to pay jobs on the basis of the sex of their incumbents would be regarded as discriminatory.

An objection could be raised that variables excluded from consideration in estimating job worth may exist that are both valid indicators of worth and correlated with percent female. Insofar as such variables exist, sex composition would stand as a surrogate for differences in job worth, in which case the coefficient $c$ could not be regarded as a valid measure of potential discrimination. For example, training in mathematics could be a job-related factor correlated with sex; its exclusion would cause $c$ to overstate the extent of potential discrimination. In the judgment of the committee, however, the burden should rest on the designer of the job evaluation system to identify and explicitly incorporate all factors regarded as legitimate components of pay differences between women and men, not merely to assert the possibility that including unspecified and unmeasured factors or improving the measurement of existing factors could reduce the "discrimination" coefficient $c$.[8]

One variable in particular that might usefully be added to pay prediction equations is the average experience of job incumbents. It is well known that men tend to have more occupational experience than women, and occupational experience is generally regarded as a compensable factor for individual workers. By not including a measure of the average work experience of incumbents in each occupation, an equation such as eq. 2 overstates the amount of sex-based discrimination to the extent that the average work experience of incumbents is negatively correlated with percent female. Other worker characteristics, such as educational qualifications, may also be important determinants of wages. Equation 2 could be expanded to include those characteristics of workers that are regarded as legitimate bases of pay differentials. An equation of the form

$$\hat{Y} = a + \Sigma b_i J_i + \Sigma c_j X_j + dF, \qquad (3)$$

---

[8] The approach outlined here is an example of a class of models that treat discrimination as a residual factor. The characteristic feature of such models, which have been widely applied in economics and sociology, is that they attempt to explain observed differences between groups with respect to some attribute (e.g., income) by predicting that attribute from a small number of other characteristics, then relating the residual difference between observed and predicted values to group membership, interpreting group differences in the average size and sign of the residual as evidence of discrimination.

From a technical point of view, however, the residuals estimated from such equations indicate the effect of *all* factors not explicitly measured plus any error in measurement; discrimination per se may or may not account for a large fraction of the residual variance. Interpreting the residual as indicating discrimination, then, requires either the strong—and clearly untenable—assumption that all relevant factors have been measured, and measured without error, or a determination that discrimination is likely. In our judgment, the proper interpretation in light of the evidence reviewed in Chapters 2 and 3 is to treat the unexplained differences in average pay rates between men and women and between minorities and nonminorities as indicating the probability of discriminatory processes, unless the contrary can be shown.

where the $X_j$ represent average characteristics of incumbents and the other variables are as defined above, can be interpreted in a manner identical to eq. 2. The substantive problem of determining which characteristics of workers should be regarded as legitimate bases of pay differentials corresponds to the problem of determining which aspects of job content should be regarded as legitimate bases of pay differentials. Ultimately, both determinations are matters of values. We should point out that job evaluation plans currently in use do not ordinarily include worker characteristics because these plans typically attempt to measure only the required elements of jobs. Experience that incumbents happen to have that is not required by the job is ordinarily considered irrelevant, while required experience is usually included as a job element, one of the $J_i$. If job evaluation procedures are to be used for the resolution of claims of pay discrimination, however, their usefulness would be enhanced by including those worker characteristics regarded as legitimate compensable factors.

### JOBS HELD BY WHITE MEN AS A STANDARD

We now turn to a different approach, the use of features of jobs held mainly by white men as a standard for assessing the fairness of the pay rates of other jobs. The key assumption of this approach is that white men in jobs held mainly by white men are not subject to discrimination.[9] With this assumption, the average pay rates of white men in jobs held mainly by white men can be used as an indication of the relative worth of these jobs; for this subset of jobs, then, there is an objective, market-based criterion of job worth.

In this approach one determines what features of those jobs contribute to differences in their level of compensation, using the familiar technique of regressing average pay rates on job characteristics. That is, an equation analogous to eq. 1,

$$\hat{Y}_{wm} = a + \Sigma b_i J_i,  \tag{4}$$

can be estimated for the subset of jobs held mainly by white men, where $Y_{wm}$ is the average pay rate for white male incumbents. The coefficients of such an equation can then be used to assign a job worth score to

---

[9] Discriminatory treatment of women or minorities would have the effect of driving down the pay of white men in jobs with substantial proportions of women and minorities. We know empirically that pay rates of men are negatively correlated with the percent female among incumbents of an occupation (see Chapter 2) and would expect a similar association with the proportion in an occupation who are minority workers.

every job in a firm—if it can be assumed that whatever factors differentiate the actual earnings of white men in jobs held mainly by white men also, and in equal proportion, differentiate the actual earnings of women and minorities and of white men in other jobs within a firm. The weakness of this approach is that if jobs held mainly by white men have characteristics substantially different from those held mainly by minorities or women, the coefficients from the earnings equation for jobs held mainly by white men will not be good estimates for jobs held mainly by women or minorities. This is an empirical issue that should be resolved in each specific case.

The strength of this approach is that it entirely avoids the question of what ought to be the bases of compensation—a question we regard as being a matter of values and admitting of no technical answer—and takes the marketplace as the arbiter of pay rates for that subset of jobs for which there is no suspicion that discriminatory processes affect the rates. To use the results of such an analysis as the standard of equitable compensation, one would apply the estimated coefficients to jobs held mainly by other workers and estimate the average wage or salary level that would be expected if such workers are compensated in the same way as white men in jobs held mainly by white men. The average earnings levels estimated in this way could then be compared with the actual earnings of those workers and the difference taken as a measure of possible discrimination. If the expected value is greater than the actual value, one could conclude that those workers are underpaid relative to the worth of their jobs; if the expected value is smaller than the actual value, one could conclude that they are overpaid. It would then be possible to adjust the pay rates of those jobs or workers who are substantially underpaid (or overpaid).

## USING STATISTICAL PROCEDURES TO CORRECT DISCRIMINATORY PAY RATES

It may be possible to use the sorts of models outlined in the previous sections to make adjustments in discriminatory pay rates, although mechanical application of these approaches without careful consideration of the measurement issues noted in this chapter would be ill-advised. Many other procedures for adjusting discriminatory aspects of pay differences could be devised; we have selected several as illustrations.

The first procedure is to pay each job according to its worth as determined by the job evaluation plan in use. This ensures that all jobs in a firm are compensated on the basis of the same criteria. If a firm is willing to use job evaluation ratings as the sole basis for establishing pay rates for jobs—as, for example, most steel manufacturers do for shop jobs and as the federal government does for white-collar jobs (Treiman, 1979)—and if the job evaluation system is free of bias, this procedure may be satisfactory.

A major disadvantage of this procedure, however, which we have noted several times above, is that, since the factor weights are usually derived in such a way as to maximize the prediction of existing pay rates and since pay rates may be strongly correlated with the sex composition of jobs, those factors most strongly correlated with sex composition may receive the heaviest weights. To the extent that this is the case, any sex bias in pay rates will tend to be preserved. To overcome this disadvantage, we suggest two modifications to the procedure.

The first modification is to use factor weights derived for white men in jobs held mainly by white men as the standard applied to all jobs. This technique has the advantage of adjusting all pay rates to a level commensurate with the highest returns currently offered, which is probably psychologically preferable but has the corresponding disadvantage of increasing the cost of the total pay package (unless, of course, the pay rates for all jobs are reduced by some constant). This technique has another disadvantage: factor weights chosen to differentiate among jobs held mainly by white men may not differentiate well among other jobs.

The second modification is to adjust the weights to remove sex composition as a compensable factor and to use the adjusted weights to develop a "bias-free" job evaluation plan. Formally this involves computing an expected income for each occupation by substituting the mean percent female over all jobs into eq. 2 (or eq. 3) and evaluating the equation. That is, for each job, $j$, a fair pay rate, $Y_j$, can be estimated by

$$\hat{Y}_j = a + \Sigma b_i' J_{ij} + c(\overline{F}),  \tag{5}$$

where $J_{ij}$ is the score on the $i$th factor for the $j$th job, and $\overline{F}$ is the mean percent female for all jobs in a firm. This technique has the advantage of adjusting the coefficients $b_i'$ to estimate the contribution of each factor to total earnings among jobs that have the same percent female.

The conventional job evaluation procedure and its modifications are similar in that they determine earnings entirely on the basis of a weighted sum of compensable factors. In this sense they are all versions of a comparable worth approach. An employer may feel, however, that such an approach is overly deterministic. After all, a variety of idiosyncratic factors may legitimately create pay differences among jobs and, it could be argued, these ought not to be ignored or arbitrarily omitted. Hence, we suggest another procedure, which preserves differences in the pay rates of jobs insofar as the unmeasured idiosyncratic components of pay differentials are uncorrelated with sex composition.

This second procedure makes use of the coefficient of percent female in eq. 2 (or eq. 3) as an adjustment factor, adding to the existing pay rate of each job a constant equal to $-c(F_j)$ or, to keep the total wage cost unchanged, $-c(F_j - \overline{F})$, where $F_j$ is the percent female in the $j$th job, $\overline{F}$ is the mean percent female for all jobs in a firm, and $c$ is the associated net regression coefficient. That is, $-c$ dollars are added to the pay rate of each job for each additional percent female among the incumbents. The result of such a procedure is to reduce the net effect of sex composition to zero. Of course, since the legitimate compensable factors will typically be correlated with sex composition, the resulting zero-order correlation between sex composition and earnings ordinarily will not be exactly zero, although it usually will be reduced.

The basic difference between the first procedure and its modifications and the second is that the former adjust all pay rates to the policy line defined by a job evaluation formula, while the latter permits pay rates to vary around the policy line, with a sole constraint: the deviations from the policy line must be uncorrelated with the sex composition of occupational categories.

With the exception of the use of unadjusted job evaluation scores as the basis for setting pay rates, these procedures have seldom been implemented, so it is difficult to anticipate what practical difficulties may be involved. Hence it would seem prudent to exercise considerable caution in applying them, attending carefully both to the statistical issues discussed above and to substantive concerns—the possibility that some workers may perceive new inequities as replacing old ones, that to avoid such perceptions may require a substantial increase in the wage bill for an enterprise, and that statistical adjustment procedures often generate tension between the need to eliminate discrimination for groups in the aggregate and the need to protect the rights of individuals. Despite these caveats, we urge the exploration of these and similar procedures as a means of eliminating discrimination in pay rates for all workers.

## CONCLUSION

Starting from the evidence that existing occupational pay hierarchies sometimes embody discriminatory elements, this chapter proposes and reviews several approaches to detecting and correcting discrimination in pay rates. These approaches are of two kinds: one involves improvements in the design and implementation of job evaluation plans currently in use and the other involves statistical adjustments to pay rates to estimate and remove the effect of the sex, race, and ethnic composition of job categories on their pay rates. Both kinds of approaches depend on two assumptions: that the basis on which jobs are paid at different rates can be made largely explicit and measurable, and that whatever cannot be measured does not favor any sex, race, or ethnic group. These assumptions seem to us to represent useful foundations for the design of methods to assess the fairness of existing pay rates within a firm. The approaches reviewed here and the procedures we illustrate are at present, however, not very well developed and are almost completely untested. Hence, it is not possible to recommend any of them unequivocally at this time.

We prefer to encourage experimentation with and exploration of the properties of these approaches in order to determine their usefulness in eliminating discrimination in pay rates. In particular, efforts should be made to improve job evaluation techniques. Research on the possibility that stereotypes are operating in the evaluation of jobs as well as research on the actual characteristics of jobs held by different groups is extremely important in improving job evaluation systems. In addition, further research on the discriminatory components of pay rates is needed. It is important to note, however, that we do not recommend requiring the installation of a job evaluation plan in a firm not using one in an attempt to ensure that the firm's pay system is nondiscriminatory. At present we know of no method that would guarantee a "fair" pay system.

# 5 Conclusions

This report has been concerned with two questions: To what extent does the fact that women and minorities are on the average paid less than nonminority men reflect discrimination in the way jobs are compensated? If wage discrimination exists, what can be done about it? On the basis of a review of the evidence, our judgment is that there is substantial discrimination in pay. Specific instances of discrimination are neither easily identified nor easily remedied, because the widespread concentration of women and minorities into low-paying jobs makes it difficult to distinguish discriminatory from nondiscriminatory components of compensation. One approach, which needs further development but shows some promise, is to use existing job evaluation plans as a standard for comparing the relative worth of jobs.

This chapter summarizes the evidence leading to these conclusions. In reviewing this material three considerations should be kept in mind.

First, discrimination, as the term is used in this report, does not imply intent but refers only to outcome. Wage discrimination exists insofar as workers of one sex, race, or ethnic group are paid less than workers of another sex, race, or ethnic group for doing work that is of "comparable," that is, equal, worth to their employer.

Second, the report has focused most intensively on sex discrimination because the issue of comparable worth arises largely in connection with job segregation, the propensity for men and women and for minority and nonminority workers to hold different sorts of jobs, and job segregation is more pronounced by sex than by race or ethnicity. Moreover, while most available data are at the national level, minorities, because of their numbers and geographical distribution, are more likely to be concentrated in particular occupations at a local level. We have therefore not been able to examine differentials by race or ethnic group with the same procedures we used to examine differentials by sex. In addition, most of the available studies of patterns of employment within firms refer to differences between men and women. Finally, the available analyses relating to the relative worth of jobs pertain almost entirely to sex discrimination. In this context, the fact that we focus mainly on discrimination based on sex should not be interpreted to mean that the committee has judged discrimination based on race or ethnicity to be of lesser importance.

Third, we have not been able to make any assessment of what the social and economic consequences may be of implementing wage policies based on the principle of equal pay for jobs of equal worth. This is an extremely complex question, with no clear answers, which goes well beyond the charge to the committee. We do, however, want to call attention to the need to give careful thought to the possible impact of implementation of a policy of equal pay for jobs of equal worth on the economic viability of firms as well as on employment opportunities for women and minorities.

## THE EXTENT AND THE SOURCES OF PAY DIFFERENTIALS

It is well established that in the United States today women earn less than men and minority men earn less than nonminority men. Among year-round full-time workers, the annual earnings of white women in the late 1970s averaged less than 60 percent of those of white men, while the earnings of black men averaged 70–75 percent of those of white men.

Such differential earnings patterns have existed for many decades. They may arise in part because women and minority men are paid less than white men for doing the same (or very similar) jobs within the same firm, or in part because the job structure is substantially segregated by sex, race, and ethnicity and the jobs held mainly by women and minority men pay less than the jobs held mainly by nonminority men. Since passage of the Equal Pay Act of 1963 and Title VII of the 1964 Civil Rights Act, legal remedies have been available for the first source of wage differentials. Although the committee recognizes that instances of unequal pay for the same work have not been entirely eliminated, we believe that they are probably not now the major source of differences in earnings.

With respect to the second source of wage differentials, the disparate distribution of workers among jobs and the concentration of women and minority men in low-paying jobs, the data are clear. Women and minorities are differentially concentrated not only by occupation but also by industry, by firm, and by division within firms. Moreover, the evidence shows that this differential concentration has persisted, at least with respect to women, over a substantial period of time. In the face of this differential concentration, then, the question of whether pay differentials are discriminatory can be stated quite simply: Would the low-paying jobs be low-paying regardless of who held them, or are they low-paying because of the sex, race, or ethnic composition of their incumbents?

To be able to state the question simply, however, is not to be able to answer it simply. In the committee's judgment, a correct response recognizes that both elements account for observed earnings differentials. Our economy is structured so that some jobs will inevitably pay less than others, and the fact that many such jobs are disproportionately filled by women and minorities may reflect differences in qualifications, interests, traditional roles, and similar factors; or it may reflect exclusionary practices with regard to hiring and promotion; or it may reflect a combination of both. However, several types of evidence support our judgment that it is also true in many instances that jobs held mainly by women and minorities pay less at least in part *because* they are held mainly by women and minorities. First, the differentials in average pay for jobs held mainly by women and those held mainly by men persist when the characteristics of jobs thought to affect their value and the characteristics of workers thought to affect their productivity are held constant. Second, prior to the legislation of the last two decades, differentials in pay for men and women and for minorities and nonminorities were often acceptable and were, in fact, prevalent. The tradition embodied in such practices was built into wage structures, and its effects continue to influence these structures. Finally, at the level of the specific firm, several studies show that women's jobs are paid less on the average than men's jobs with the same scores derived from job evaluation plans. The evidence is not complete or conclusive, but the consistency of the results in many different job categories and in several different types of studies, the size of the pay differentials (even after worker and job characteristics have been taken into account), and the lack of evidence for alternative explanations strongly suggest that wage discrimination is widespread.

## IDENTIFYING AND ELIMINATING PAY DISCRIMINATION

The identification and correction of particular instances of pay discrimination are, however, not easy tasks. One procedure that has been suggested is to compare the actual rates of pay of jobs with the relative worth of jobs; wage discrimination would be suspected whenever jobs are not paid in accordance with their relative worth. This relative (or comparable) worth approach in turn requires a generally acceptable standard of job worth and a feasible procedure for measuring the relative worth of jobs. In our judgment no universal standard of job worth exists, both because any definition of the "relative worth" of jobs is in part a matter of values and because, even for a particular definition, problems of measurement are likely.

One approach to the relative worth of jobs avoids the issue of values by equating the worth of jobs with existing pay rates. In this approach, no comparable worth strategy is needed to adjust the pay rates of jobs, because the pay rates themselves reflect the relative worth of jobs. The belief that existing pay differentials between jobs provide a valid measure of the relative worth of jobs depends on the view that the operation of labor markets is freely competitive and that pay differentials primarily reflect differences in individual productivity and are not substantially influenced by discrimination. While there is a good deal of controversy about the nature of labor markets, in our view the operation of labor markets can be better understood as reflecting a variety of institutions that limit competition with respect to workers and wages and tend to perpetuate whatever discrimination exists. As a result of these institutional features of labor markets, existing wage rates do not in our judgment provide a measure of the relative worth of jobs that avoids discrimination.

Several of these institutional features are inherent to the current operation of labor markets and cannot easily be altered. Substantial investment in training makes it difficult for workers to shift from one occupation to another in search of higher pay. Moreover, even within specific occupations, workers are not generally free to sell their labor to the highest bidder; they are constrained by geographical location and imperfect information as well as by institutional arrangements designed to encourage the stability of the work force by putting a premium on seniority. Nor do employers generally seek labor on the open market; a large fraction of all jobs are filled through internal promotions or transfers. Finally, both the supply of and demand for labor and the pay rates offered are strongly affected by still other forces—particularly union contracts and governmental regulations. Whenever jobs are relatively insulated from market forces, traditional differences in pay rates tend to be perpetuated over time. Hence, insofar as differences in pay between jobs ever did incorporate discriminatory elements, they tend to be perpetuated.

## JOB EVALUATION PLANS

Although no universal standard of job worth exists, job evaluation plans do provide standards and measures of job worth that are used to estimate the relative worth of jobs within many firms. In job evaluation plans, pay ranges for a job are based on estimates of the worth of jobs according to such criteria as the skill, effort, and responsibility required by the job and the working conditions under which it is performed. Pay for an individual, within the pay range, is set by the worker's characteristics, such as credentials, seniority, productivity, and quality of job performance. Job evaluation plans vary from firm to firm; both the criteria established and the compensable factors and relative weights used as measures of the criteria differ somewhat from plan to plan.

In our judgment job evaluation plans provide measures of job worth that, under certain circumstances, may be used to discover and reduce wage discrimination for persons covered by a given plan. Job evaluation plans provide a way of systematically rewarding jobs for their content— for the skill, effort, and responsibility they entail and the conditions under which they are performed. By making the criteria of compensation explicit and by applying the criteria consistently, it is probable that pay differentials resulting from traditional stereotypes regarding the value of "women's work" or work customarily done by minorities will be reduced.

But several aspects of the methods generally used in such plans raise questions about their ability to establish comparable worth. First, job evaluation plans typically ensure rough conformity between the measured worth of jobs and actual wages by allowing actual wages to determine the weights of job factors used in the plans. Insofar as differentials associated with sex, race, or ethnicity are incorporated in actual wages, this procedure will act to perpetuate them. Statistical techniques exist that may be able to generate job worth scores from which components of wages associated with sex, race, or ethnicity have been at least partly removed; they should be further developed.

Second, many firms use different job evaluation plans for different types of jobs. Since in most firms women and minority men are concentrated in jobs with substantially different tasks from those of jobs held by nonminority men, a plan that covers all jobs would be necessary in order to compare wages of women, minority men, and nonminority men. The selection of compensable factors and their weights in such a plan may be quite difficult, however, because factors appropriate for one type of job are not necessarily appropriate for all other types. Nevertheless, experiments with firm-wide plans might be useful in making explicit the relative weights of compensable factors, especially since they are already used by some firms.

Finally, it must be recognized that there are no definitive tests of the "fairness" of the choice of compensable factors and the relative weights given to them. The process is inherently judgmental and its success in generating a wage structure that is deemed equitable depends on achieving a consensus about factors and their weights among employers and employees.

The development and implementation of a job evaluation plan is often a lengthy and costly process. The underdeveloped nature of the technology involved, particularly the lack of systematic testing of assumptions, does not justify the universal application of such plans. In the committee's judgment, however, the plans have a potential that deserves further experimentation and development.

# References

Allison, Elisabeth K.
  1976   "Sex linked earning differentials in the beauty industry." Journal of Human Resources 11 (Summer):383–90.
Astin, Helen S., Allison Parelman, and Ann Fisher
  1975   Sex Roles: A Research Bibliography. Rockville, Md.: National Institute of Mental Health.
Astin, Helen S., Nancy Suniewick, and Susan Dweck
  1971   Women: A Bibliography on Their Education and Careers. Washington, D.C.: Human Services Press. (Reprinted in 1975 by Behavioral Publications, New York.)
Baron, Harold
  1971   "The demand for black labor." Radical America 5 (March and April):1–46.
Baron, Harold, and Bennett Hymer
  1968   "The Negro in the Chicago labor market." In Julius Jacobsen (ed.), The Negro and the American Labor Movement. New York: Doubleday (Anchor Books).
Barrett, Nancy S.
  1979   "Women in the job market: occupations, earnings, and career opportunities." Pp. 31–61 in Ralph E. Smith (ed.), The Subtle Revolution: Women at Work. Washington, D.C.: The Urban Institute.
Beck, E. M., Patrick M. Horan, and Charles M. Tolbert
  1978   "Stratification in a dual economy: a sectoral model of earnings determination." American Sociological Review 43 (October):704–20.
  1980a  "Industrial segmentation and labor market discrimination." Social Problems 28 (December):113–30.
  1980b  "Reply to Hauser, 'Social stratification in industrial society: further evidence for a structural alternative.'" American Sociological Review 45 (August):712–18.
Becker, Gary S.
  1957   The Economics of Discrimination. First Edition. Chicago: University of Chicago Press.
  1971   The Economics of Discrimination. Second Edition. Chicago: University of Chicago Press.

*97*

1975    Human Capital: A Theoretical and Empirical Analysis, With Special Reference
        to Education. Second Edition. New York: National Bureau of Economic Re-
        search.
Bergmann, Barbara R.
1971    "The effects on white incomes of discrimination in employment." Journal of
        Political Economy 79 (March/April):294–313.
1974    "Occupational segregation, wages and profits when employers discriminate by
        race or sex." Eastern Economic Journal 1 (April/July):103–10.
Bibb, Robert, and William H. Form
1977    "The effects of industrial, occupational, and sex stratification on wages in blue-
        collar markets." Social Forces 55 (June):974–96.
Bickner, Mei Liang
1974    Women at Work: An Annotated Bibliography. Los Angeles: University of
        California, Institute of Industrial Relations, Manpower Research Center.
Birnbaum, Michael H.
1979    "Procedures for the detection and correction of salary inequities." Pp. 121–44
        in T. R. Pezzullo and B. E. Brittingham (eds.), Salary Equity: Detecting Sex
        Bias in Salaries Among College and University Professors. Lexington, Mass.:
        Lexington Books.
Blau, Francine D.
1977    Equal Pay in the Office. Lexington, Mass.: Lexington Books.
Blau, Francine D., and Carol L. Jusenius
1976    "Economists' approaches to sex segregation in the labor market: an appraisal."
        Pp. 181–99 in Martha Blaxall and Barbara Reagan (eds.), Women and the
        Workplace: The Implications of Occupational Segregation. Chicago: University
        of Chicago Press.
Bluestone, Barry
1970    "The tripartite economy: labor markets and the working poor." Poverty and
        Human Resource Abstracts 5 (July/August):15–35.
Bluestone, Barry, William M. Murphy, and Mary H. Stevenson
1973    Low Wages and the Working Poor. Ann Arbor, Mich.: University of Michigan,
        Institute of Labor and Industrial Relations.
Bridges, William P., and Richard A. Berk
1974    "Determinants of white-collar income: an evaluation of equal pay for equal
        work." Social Science Research 3 (September):211–34.
Buchele, Robert
1976    "Jobs and workers: a labor market segmentation perspective on the work ex-
        perience of middle-aged men." Unpublished paper submitted to the Secretary
        of Labor's Conference on the National Longitudinal Survey of the Pre-Retire-
        ment Years, Boston.
Buckley, J.
1971    "Pay differences between men and women in the same job." Monthly Labor
        Review 94 (November):36–39.
Cain, Glen
1976    "The challenge of segmented labor market theories to orthodox theory: a sur-
        vey." Journal of Economic Literature 14 (December):1215–57.
Chamberlain, Neil, and Donald Cullen
1971    The Labor Sector. New York: McGraw Hill.
Christensen v. Iowa
1977    563 F.2d 353, U.S. Court of Appeals for the Eighth Circuit.

Cook, Thomas D., and Donald T. Campbell
1979    "Inferring cause from passive observation." Ch. 7 in Quasi Experimentation: Design and Analysis for Field Settings. Chicago: Rand McNally.
Corcoran, Mary E.
1979    "Women's experience, labor force withdrawals, and women's wages: empirical results using the 1976 Panel of Income Dynamics." Pp. 216–45 in Cynthia B. Lloyd, Emily S. Andrews, and Curtis L. Gilroy (eds.), Women in the Labor Market. Conference on Women in the Labor Market, 1977, Barnard College. New York: Columbia University Press.
Corcoran, Mary, and Gregory J. Duncan
1979    "Work history, labor force attachment, and earnings differences between the races and sexes." Journal of Human Resources 14 (Winter):3–20.
County of Washington, Oregon, et al. v. Gunther et al.
1980    No. 80-429. Argued before the Supreme Court March 23, 1981. Decided June 8, 1981.
Darland, M. G., S. M. Dawkins, J. L. Lovasich, E. L. Scott, M. E. Sherman, and J. Z. Whipple
1973    "Applications of multivariate regression to studies of salary differences between men and women faculty." Pp. 120–32 in Proceedings of the Social Statistics Section of the American Statistical Association. Washington, D.C.: American Statistical Association.
Doeringer, Peter B., and Michael J. Piore
1971    Internal Labor Markets and Manpower Analysis. Lexington, Mass.: D.C. Heath.
Duncan, Gregory J., and Saul Hoffman
1978    "Training and earnings." Pp. 105–50 in Gregory J. Duncan and James N. Morgan (eds.), Five Thousand American Families: Patterns of Economic Progress. Vol. 6. Accounting for Race and Sex Differences in Earnings and Other Analyses of the First Nine Years of the Panel Study of Income Dynamics. Ann Arbor: Institute for Social Research, University of Michigan.
Duncan, Beverly, and Otis Dudley Duncan
1978    Sex Typing and Social Roles: A Research Report. New York: Academic Press.
Duncan, Otis Dudley, and Beverly Duncan
1955    "A methodological analysis of segregation indexes." American Sociological Review 20 (April):210–17.
Edwards, Richard C.
1977    "Personal traits and 'success' in schooling and work." Educational and Psychological Measurement 37 (Spring):125–38.
1979    Contested Terrain: The Transformation of the Workplace in America. New York: Basic Books.
England, Paula
1982    "The failure of human capital theory to explain occupational sex segregation." Journal of Human Resources. In press.
Equal Employment Opportunity Commission
1972    " 'A unique competence': a study of equal employment opportunity in the Bell system." Congressional Record, extension of remarks, February 17, pp. 4507–36.
Featherman, David L, and Robert M. Hauser
1976    "Sexual inequalities and socioeconomic achievement in the U.S., 1962-1973." American Sociological Review 41 (June):462–83.

Flanagan, Robert J.
   1976    "Actual versus potential impact of government antidiscrimination programs."
           Industrial and Labor Relations Review 29 (July):486–503.
Freeman, Richard
   1973    Black Elite: Education and Labor Market Discrimination. New York: McGraw
           Hill.
Friedman, Milton
   1971    "The supply of factors of production." Pp. 3–20 in John F. Burton, Lee K.
           Benham, William M. Vaughn, and Robert J. Flanagan (eds.), Readings in
           Labor Market Analysis. New York: Holt, Reinhart and Winston.
Fuchs, Victor
   1971    "Differences in hourly earnings between men and women." Monthly Labor
           Review 94 (May):9–15.
Galloway, Sue, and Alyce Archuleta
   1978    "Sex and salary: equal pay for comparable work." American Libraries 9
           (May):281–85.
Glenn, Evelyn Nakano
   1980    "The dialectics of wage work: Japanese-American women and domestic serv-
           ice, 1905–1940." Feminist Studies 6 (Fall):432–71.
Goldberger, Arthur S.
   1968    Topics in Regression Analysis. New York: Macmillan.
Gordon, David M.
   1972    Theories of Poverty and Underemployment. Lexington, Mass.: Lexington
           Books.
Gregory, Robert G., and Ronald C. Duncan
   1981    "The relevance of segmented labor market theories: the Australian experience
           of the achievement of equal pay for women." Journal of Post Keynesian Eco-
           nomics 3 (Spring):403–28.
Gwartney, James, and Richard Stroup
   1973    "Measurement of employment discrimination according to sex." Southern Eco-
           nomic Journal 39(April):575–87.
Hacker, Sally L.
   1978    "Sex stratification, technology and organizational change: a longitudinal analy-
           sis of AT&T." Paper presented at the Annual Meetings of the American So-
           ciological Association, San Francisco, August.
Halaby, Charles N.
   1979    "Sexual inequality in the workplace: an employer-specific analysis of pay dif-
           ferences." Social Science Research 8 (March):79–104.
Harrison, Bennett, and Andrew Sum
   1979    "The theory of 'dual' or segmented labor markets." Journal of Economic Issues
           13 (September):687–706.
Hartmann, Heidi I.
   1976    "Capitalism, patriarchy, and job segregation by sex." Signs 1 (Spring, Part
           2):137–69.
Hartmann, Heidi I., Patricia A. Roos, and Donald J. Treiman
   1980    "Strategies for assessing and correcting pay discrimination: an empirical exer-
           cise." Staff paper prepared for the Committee on Occupational Classification
           and Analysis, National Research Council, National Academy of Sciences, June.
Hauser, Robert M.
   1980    "Comment on Beck et al., ASR, October 1978, 'Stratification in a dual econ-
           omy.'" American Sociological Review 45 (August):702–11.

International Labour Office
1975 "Equal remuneration." General Survey by the Committee of Experts on the Application of Conventions and Recommendations, Report III (Part 4B). Geneva: International Labour Office.

Kahn, Lawrence M.
1976 "Internal labor markets: San Francisco longshoremen." Industrial Relations 15 (October):333–37.

Kohen, Andrew I., with Susan C. Breinich, and Patricia M. Shields
1975 "Women and the economy: a bibliography and a review of the literature on sex differentiation in the labor market." Columbus: Ohio State University, Center for Human Resource Research.

Kronstadt, Sylvia
1978 "Women v. the City of Denver: 'new frontier' for equal rights." The Nation (April 29):505–506.

Laws, Judith Long
1979 The Second X: Sex Role and Social Roles. New York: Elsevier.

Lemons, Mary, et al. v. City and County of Denver
1978 17 FEP Cases 906, 907 (The United States District Court for the District of Colorado); Civil Action No. 78-1499, U.S. Court of Appeals for the Tenth Circuit.

Levitan, Sar A., and Richard S. Belous
1979 "The minimum wage today: how well does it work?" Monthly Labor Review 102 (July):17–21.

Lucas, Robert E. B.
1977 "Hedonic wage equations and psychic wages in the returns to schooling." American Economic Review 67 (September):549–58.

Maccoby, Eleanor Emmons, and Carol Nagy Jacklin
1974 The Psychology of Sex Differences. Stanford: Stanford University Press.

Madansky, Albert
1959 "The fitting of straight lines when both variables are subject to error." Journal of the American Statistical Assocation 54(285):173–205.

Madden, Janice F.
1975 "Discrimination—a manifestation of male market power?" Pp. 146–74 in Cynthia B. Lloyd (ed.), Sex, Discrimination, and the Divison of Labor. New York: Columbia University Press.

Malkiel, B. G., and J. A. Malkiel
1973 "Male-female pay differentials in professional employment." American Economic Review 63 (September):693–705.

McCormick, Ernest J., and D. R. Ilgen
1980 Industrial Psychology. Seventh Edition. Englewood Cliffs, N.J.: Prentice-Hall.

McNulty, D.
1967 "Difference in pay between men and women workers." Monthly Labor Review 90 (December):40–43.

Mednick, Martha T. Shuch, Sandra Schwartz Tangri, and Lois Wladis Hoffman (eds.)
1975 Women and Achievement: Social and Motivational Analysis. New York: Wiley (Halsted Press).

Miller, Ann R., Donald J. Treiman, Pamela S. Cain, and Patricia A. Roos (eds.)
1980 Work, Jobs, and Occupations: A Critical Review of The Dictionary of Occupational Titles. Report of the Committee on Occupational Classification and Analysis to the U.S. Department of Labor. Washington, D.C.: National Academy Press.

Mincer, Jacob
  1970    "The distribution of labor incomes: a survey with special reference to the human
          capital approach." Journal of Economic Literature 8 (March):1–26.
Mincer, Jacob, and Solomon W. Polachek
  1974    "Family investments in human capital: earnings of women." Journal of Political
          Economy 82 (March/April, Part II):S76–S108.
  1978    "Women's earnings reexamined." Journal of Human Resources 13 (Win-
          ter):118–34.
Mosteller, Frederick, and John W. Tukey
  1977    Data Analysis and Regression: A Second Course in Statistics. Reading, Mass.:
          Addison-Wesley.
Newman, Winn
  1976    "Combatting occupational segregation: presentation iii." Pp. 265–72 in Martha
          Blaxall and Barbara Reagan (eds.), Women and the Workplace: The Impli-
          cations of Occupational Segregation. Chicago: University of Chicago Press.
Oaxaca, Ronald
  1973    "Sex discrimination in wages." Pp. 124–51 in Orley Ashenfelter and Albert
          Rees (eds.), Discrimination in Labor Markets. Princeton, N.J.: Princeton
          University Press.
Oppenheimer, Valerie K.
  1970    The Female Labor Force in the United States: Demographic and Economic
          Factors Governing Its Growth and Changing Composition. Westport, Conn.:
          Greenwood Press.
Osterman, Paul
  1978    "Sex, marriage, children, and statistical discrimination." Discussion paper no.
          16. Department of Economics, Boston University.
Perlman, Nancy D., and Bruce J. Ennis
  1980    "Preliminary memorandum on pay equity: achieving equal pay for work of
          comparable value." Albany: State University of New York, Center for Women
          in Government.
Phelps, Edmund S.
  1972    "The statistical theory of racism and sexism." American Economic Review 62
          (September):659–66.
Phelps-Brown, E. H.
  1977    The Inequality of Pay. Berkeley: University of California Press.
Piore, Michael J. (ed.)
  1979    Unemployment and Inflation: Institutional and Structuralist Views. White
          Plains, N.Y.: M. E. Sharpe, Inc.
Polachek, Solomon
  1976    "Occupational segregation: an alternative hypothesis." Journal of Contempo-
          rary Business 5 (Winter):1–12.
  1979    "Occupational segregation among women: theory, evidence, and a prognosis."
          Pp. 137–57 in Cynthia B. Lloyd, Emily S. Andrews, and Curtis L. Gilroy (eds.),
          Women in the Labor Market. Conference on Women in the Labor Market,
          1977, Barnard College. New York: Columbia University Press.
Rees, Albert, and George P. Shultz
  1970    Workers and Wages in an Urban Labor Market. Chicago: University of Chicago
          Press.
Reich, Michael
  1978    "Who benefits from racism? The distribution among whites of gains and losses

from racial inequality." Journal of Human Resources 13 (Fall):524–44.
1981 Racial Inequality: A Political Economic Analysis. Princeton, N.J.: Princeton University Press.
Remick, Helen
1978 "Strategies for creating sound, bias free job evaluation plans." In Job Evaluation and EEO: The Emerging Issues. New York: Industrial Relations Counselors, Inc.
1980 "Beyond equal pay for equal work: comparable worth in the State of Washington." Pp. 405–48 in Ronnie Steinberg Ratner (ed.), Equal Employment Policy for Women: Strategies for Implementation in the United States, Canada, and Western Europe. Philadelphia: Temple University Press.
Roos, Patricia A.
1981 "Sex stratification in the workplace: male-female differences in economic returns to occupation." Social Science Research 10(3).
Rosen, Sherwin
1974 "Hedonic prices and implicit markets: product differentiation in pure competition." Journal of Political Economy 82 (January/February):34–55.
Rumberger, Russell W., and Martin Carnoy
1980 "Segmentation in the US labour market: its effects on the mobility and earnings of whites and blacks." Cambridge Journal of Economics 4 (June):117–32.
Sanborn, H.
1964 "Pay differences between men and women." Industrial and Labor Relations Review 17 (July):534–50.
Sawhill, Isabel V.
1973 "The economics of discrimination against women: some new findings." Journal of Human Resources 8 (Summer):383–96.
Scanzoni, John H.
1975 Sex Roles, Life Styles and Childbearing: Changing Patterns in Marriage and the Family. New York: Free Press.
Schlei, Barbara Lindemann, and Paul Grossman
1976 Employment Discrimination Law. (Supplement 1979). Washington, D.C.: Bureau of National Affairs.
Schultz, T. W.
1961 "Investment in human capital." American Economic Review 51 (March):1–17.
Scott, W. Richard
1979 "Measuring outputs in hospitals." Pp. 276–308 in National Research Council, Measurement and Interpretation of Productivity. Panel to Review Productivity Statistics, Committee on National Statistics. Washington, D.C.: National Academy of Sciences.
Smith, James P., and Finis R. Welch
1977 "Black-white male wage ratios: 1960–70." American Economic Review 67 (June):323–38.
Smith, Ralph E.
1979 "The movement of women into the labor force." Pp. 1–29 in Ralph E. Smith (ed.), The Subtle Revolution: Women at Work. Washington, D.C.: The Urban Institute.
Smith, Robert
1979 "Compensating wage differentials and public policy: a review." Industrial and Labor Relations Review 32 (April):339–51.

Sommers, Dixie
1974    "Occupational rankings for men and women by earnings." Monthly Labor
        Review 97 (August):34–51.
Stevenson, Mary H.
1973    "Women's wages and job segregation." Politics and Society 4 (Fall):83–96.
1974    "Determinants of low wages for women workers." Unpublished PhD disser-
        tation. University of Michigan.
1975    "Relative wages and sex segregation by occupation." Pp. 175–200 in Cynthia
        Lloyd (ed.), Sex, Discrimination, and the Division of Labor. New York: Col-
        umbia University Press.
1978    "Wage differences between men and women: economic theories." Pp. 89–107
        in Ann H. Stromberg and Shirley Harkness (eds.), Women Working. Palo Alto,
        Calif.: Mayfield.
Stolzenberg, Ross M.
1979    "The measurement and decomposition of causal effects in nonlinear and non-
        additive models." Pp. 459–88 in Karl F. Schuessler (ed.), Sociological Meth-
        odology 1980. San Francisco: Jossey-Bass.
Stone, Katherine
1975    "The origins of job structures in the steel industry." Pp. 27–84 in Richard C.
        Edwards, Michael Reich, and David M. Gordon (eds.), Labor Market Seg-
        mentation. Lexington, Mass.: D.C. Health.
Suter, Larry, and Herman Miller
1973    "Income differences between men and women." American Journal of Sociology
        78 (January):962–74.
Talbert, Joan, and Christine E. Bose
1977    "Wage attainment processes: the retail clerk case." American Journal of So-
        ciology 33 (September):403–24.
Thurow, Lester C.
1969    Poverty and Discrimination. Washington, D.C.: Brookings Institution.
1975    Generating Inequality. New York: Basic Books.
Treiman, Donald J.
1973    "Occupational differences in marriage and childbearing among women: an an-
        alytic strategy." Paper given at the Workshop on Women's Roles and Fertility,
        National Institute of Child Health and Human Development, Belmont, Md.,
        December.
1977    Occupational Prestige in Comparative Perspective. New York: Academic Press.
1979    Job Evaluation: An Analytic Review. Interim Report of the Committee on
        Occupational Classification and Analysis to the Equal Employment Opportunity
        Commission. National Research Council. Washington, D.C.: National Acad-
        emy of Sciences.
Treiman, Donald J., and Kermit Terrell
1975a   "Sex and the process of status attainment: a comparison of working women and
        men." American Sociological Review 40 (April):174–200.
1975b   "Women, work, and wages—trends in the female occupational structure since
        1940." Pp. 157–200 in Kenneth C. Land and Seymour Spilerman (eds.), Social
        Indicator Models. New York: Russell Sage Foundation.
Tyler, Gus
1978    "The other economy." The New Leader, May 8.
U.S. Bureau of the Census
1973    Census of Population: 1970. Subject Reports. Final Report PC(2)-7A, Occu-

pational Characteristics. Washington, D.C.: U.S. Government Printing Office.

1979 County Business Patterns 1977. United States. Washington, D.C.: U.S. Government Printing Office.

1980 Money income of families and persons in the United States, 1978. Current Population Reports, Series P-60, No. 118. Washington, D.C.: U.S. Government Printing Office.

U.S. Commission on Civil Rights

1978 Social Indicators of Equality for Minorities and Women. Washington, D.C.: U.S. Commission on Civil Rights.

U.S. Department of Labor, Bureau of Labor Statistics

1977 U.S. Working Women: A Databook, Bulletin 1977. Washington, D.C.: U.S. Government Printing Office.

1980a Area Wage Survey: Newark, New Jersey Metropolitan Area, January, 1980. Bulletin 3000-8. Washington, D.C.: U.S. Government Printing Office.

1980b Employment and Earnings 27 (January). Washington, D.C.: U.S. Department of Labor.

U.S. Department of Labor, Employment Standards Administration

1978 Minimum Wage and Maximum Hours Standards Under the Fair Labor Standards Act. An Economic Effects Study Submitted to Congress in 1978. Washington, D.C.: U.S. Department of Labor.

U.S. Department of Labor, Women's Bureau

1969 Summary of State Labor Laws for Women. Washington, D.C.: U.S. Government Printing Office.

Wachter, Michael L.

1975 "Primary and secondary labor markets: a critique of the dual approach." Pp. 637–93 in Arthur M. Okun and George L. Perry (eds.), Brookings Papers in Economic Analysis. Vol. 3. Washington, D.C.: Brookings Institution.

Ward, Virginia L.

1980 "Measuring wage relationships among selected occupations." Monthly Labor Review 103 (May):21–25.

Welch, Finis

1973 "Education and racial discrimination." Pp. 43–81 in Orley Ashenfelter and Albert Rees (eds.), Discrimination in Labor Markets. Princeton, N.J.: Princeton University Press.

Willis, Norman D., and Associates

1974 State of Washington Comparable Worth Study. Seattle: Norman D. Willis and Associates.

1976 State of Washington Comparable Worth Study. Phase II. Seattle: Norman D. Willis and Associates.

Women Library Workers and the Commission on the Status of Women

1978 Comparable Pay Study of the City and County of San Francisco. San Francisco: Women Library Workers and the Commission on the Status of Women.

Wootton, Barbara A.

1955 The Social Foundations of Wage Policy. London: Allen and Unwin.

# Supplementary Statement

GUS TYLER

Although in full agreement with the primary thrust of the committee report, I am submitting this separate, albeit concurring, opinion for inclusion as an addendum. I am impelled to do so because the report, committed as it is to responding to the formal charge, does not offer an adequate strategy to cope with a continuing inequity in the wage and salary structure of the nation; namely, the gap between the average earnings of men and women.

The formal charge was to "study the principles and procedures used in determining compensation for work in the United States" with a special eye on discriminatory practices, based on sex, race, or national origin. What the committee found was a vast variety of systems, with a crazy quilt of criteria, whose ultimate outcome—for the society as a whole—showed women earning substantially less than men although the attributes required to do their work were, on the average, comparable.

The report finds that an important reason for this wage differential is the ghettoization of women in the economy, their concentration in occupations, trades, and professions in which compensation is relatively low; and, within other categories, concentration in subclassifications in which compensation is low. Chapters 1, 2, and 3 of the report spell out and substantiate these findings and conclusions. Chapter 4 addresses

*Note:* Mary C. Dunlap concurs with this statement.

*107*

itself to wage adjustment strategies, an attempt to right the wrong. Here two approaches are offered for detecting discrimination "within a single firm."

Although the elimination of discrimination "within a single firm" is desirable and, in some cases, the remedy discussed may yield substantial results, the primary problem of women in the American economy does not arise from intra-plant inequities, but from the maldistribution of women in the total economy. The report does not address itself to this latter and crucial question—as it probably could not in view of its limited charge. It is for this reason that I asked the indulgence of the committee in permitting me these *obiter dicta* on proposed strategies to deal with the central problem of wage differentials between men and women in the society as a whole.

I did not urge these strategies on the committee because they involve political, legislative, and union actions that are, by their nature, controversial and beyond the scope of the committee's defined jurisdiction. Nevertheless, at a time when women—and others—are seeking greater wage and salary equity, I believe it is a valuable public service to offer the following commentary as a contribution to a fruitful public dialogue.

The key data on what has been happening to women in the economy are contained in Table 3, which shows the median annual income for full-time workers, tabulated by sex and race. It shows that white women are falling ever further behind white men. In 1955, the average income of white women was 65.3 percent of that of white men; by 1977, white women were earning only 57.7 percent as much as white men. The decline in relative earnings of women was not sudden; it has been a slow continuing downward crawl, with slight oscillations along the descending line.

How can we explain this decline in wages of the American working woman? If we ascribe the worsening status to "discrimination," then we must conclude that pay discrimination against women is more severe today than a full generation ago.

Such a conclusion, however, is believing what we are not seeing. Since the mid-1960s, equal pay for equal work has been the law—and has been enforced. The law has also been interpreted to require equal pay for very similar work. In many cases, workers—generally through their unions—have even been able to win comparable pay for "comparable work" *within plants*. Women also legally have equal access to jobs. In the light of all this, it seems commonsensically improbable that the growing gap between the wages of white women and white men is due to growing "discrimination" against women workers.

The attempt to assign the cause primarily or exclusively to discrimination is further cast into doubt when we examine the relationship between the wages of *black women* and *white men*. In the last generation, black women have decisively improved their status vis-a-vis white men. In 1955, black women earned about one-third as much as white men; by 1977, they were earning more than half as much. As a consequence the earnings of black women have risen from about 50 percent of those of white women in 1955 to almost 95 percent in 1977.

A final anomaly is the rise in earnings of black male workers vis-a-vis white male workers—from about 60 percent in 1955 to more than 70 percent in 1977.

If we limit our search for cause solely to pay discrimination, we must conclude that discrimination against black men and women (especially women) was easing at a time when discrimination against white women was intensifying. If that seems uncomfortably odd, then we must look for other explanations of our data.

The simplest explanation lies in the changing mix of employment in the American economy over the last generation. The great expansion in the economy has been in those sectors in which pay is and traditionally has been relatively low—primarily (although not exclusively) in the service sectors. It is precisely these lower-paying sectors that women have been entering in vast numbers as they leave their chores at home for employment in the labor market. The higher the percentage of women in the service and other low-paying sectors, the lower is their average wage as contrasted with that of men. The same explanation applies to the rise of black women workers. Many of those who were once employed as domestics—among the lowest-paying of all trades—have moved into labor-intensive manufacture and service jobs in which wages are low but still higher than those of household workers. In addition, millions of black women have relocated their employment from rural small town areas to urban centers where wages and salaries are higher. As the jobs that black women hold become increasingly the same as those that white women hold, black women tend to earn the same as white women. The same explanation also applies to the improved relative wage of black men, many of whom—in the last generation—have moved into construction, capital-intensive manufacture, and public employment, including posts of professional status.

If this explanation of wage differentials for four major groups in society—white men, white women, black men, and black women—is valid, then the basic cause for the rising and falling gaps is not some malfunctioning job evaluation system in a plant but the maldistribution of these populations in the American economy.

Theoretically, this maldistribution should be self-correcting once there is equal access to jobs—regardless of race, creed, color, sex, age, or national origin. But, as the committee report so ably explains, there are endless institutional barriers—geographic, psychologic, social, organizational, etc.—to the easy flow of individuals from one sector or subdivision of the economy to another. For "equal access" to provide the ultimate remedy may require many generations.

What is more, if the working population were redistributed, the prevailing inequities in pay would not be eliminated or even lessened: present injustices would merely be integrated by sex. An equal percentage of women and men would now be consigned to the under-tier of our economy, to what in another essay I called "the other economy." Changing the sex, race, or national origin of the denizens of darkness does not bring light to those imprisoned in the smelly underbelly of our economy.

As the years go by, we may expect that the gap between those in the top tier and those in the lower tier of the economy (heavily female and minority) will grow. Workers in the first tier not only have higher hourly wages, but they also get a higher percentage of fringe benefits on their high hourly base; workers in the second tier have lower hourly wages (50 percent less) and get a much smaller percentage in fringe benefits on their smaller base.

Periods of inflation widen the gap rapidly. Workers in the first tier are more or less able to negotiate contracts or bargain individually to keep up with rising prices: their employers are richer, more oligopolized, and sufficiently capital-intensive so as not to worry too much about pay levels to their key personnel. Workers in the second tier are unable to keep up: their employers are poorer, smaller, buffeted by competition, and dependent on labor-intensive production. The other difference is the degree of unionization—the upper tier is much more highly organized than the lower tier. The result is that workers in the upper tier are able to keep up or even improve their real earnings in periods of inflation while workers in the lower tier fall further behind each year.

If, then, redistribution of workers within the present economy is not the answer and if the present trend is toward a growing disparity in the income of workers in the two tiers, what strategies for greater equity can we pursue to offer some hope to the women (and minorities) trapped in the lower depths? The following are a few suggestions.

## Minimum Wage

The construction of a sturdy minimum wage as a foundation for wages (and for our economy) is so basic that the process ought to be only minimally a legislative function that depends on the composition or the calendar of a current Congress. The minimum wage ought to be indexed at something like 60 percent of the average manufacturing wage, operating like a cost-of-living adjustment clause in a labor-management contract. (In fact, 60 percent is less than 60 percent because of the differences in fringe benefits.)

Such a minimum wage should apply to all workers, regardless of race, sex, or age. To create a youth subminimum or an aged subminimum or a female subminimum is just a form of discrimination in employment directed against the more vulnerable elements in the population. If certain workers deserve more because they perform better, they should be paid more by lifting them above the minimum and not by paying others less by depressing the minimum for the weakest categories of workers.

## Import Regulation

A second measure to allow workers in labor-intensive manfacture to elevate their wages is the regulaton of imports. Competition from countries where the wages may run as low as one-tenth the wage of the American worker keeps the domestic rate unnecessarily low.

The loss of jobs in labor-intensive manufacture is considerable and is clearly not balanced by a growth of jobs in capital-intensive manufacture, such as steel and auto, where jobs are also threatened by imports.

To regulate imports requires tariffs, quotas, and revision of the tax law to remove inducements for American manufacturers to produce overseas. It is particularly important to repeal Item 807 of the Tariff Code that actively encourages American companies to contract out much of their work to other countries. Item 807 reduces the tariff on goods that are assembled in other lands if the component parts originate in the United States. In the apparel industry, for example, that means that if a company sends out goods across the border or overseas to be stitched, it may then bring the finished product back into the United States, while paying a very limited tariff merely on value added—a sum that in low-wage countries is negligible.

It is vain to expect that American companies will overcome the import threat by improvements in American productivity, design, or merchandising. Most of the goods coming from abroad are manufactured under American auspices, with American companies supplying the design, the methods of production, and the merchandising. American brand names are inserted overseas since, in many cases, the total output of the overseas "contractor" is committed to an American manufacturer or retailer. Contracting work overseas is a way of holding down the pay of workers in manufacturing in the United States.

## Plant Removal Regulation

This widespread practice leads to the closing of American plants, either to open a similar plant in some low-wage country overseas or to contract out the work, once done by an American contractor, to a foreign contractor.

For workers employed in light labor-intensive manufacture such overseas plant removal is but the continuation of a long history of "runaway" factories. In the past, such factories have generally run away from higher-wage to lower-wage areas within the United States. While such removals have caused considerable instability in employment and wage standards, the movements have been confined within the American ambience of minimum wages, child labor laws, occupational safety guidelines, equal employment opportunities, etc. But when a plant moves overseas, it is exempt from all the civilizing circumstances of our American culture and, in addition, is generally removed from union organization in lands that often forbid free unionism. The mere threat to move production overseas is a simple way to hold down the wage of the American worker in light manufacturing.

While the problem of plant removal is a threat to all American manufacturing—hitting communities as well as employees—light industry is more susceptible than heavy industry because there is a smaller investment by labor-intensive production in fixed capital. For that reason, new legislation is required to cope with the growing threat of plant removal.

## Labor-Management Act Reform

Just as plant removal hits labor-intensive industry harder than capital-intensive industry, so too does the deterioration of the Wagner Labor-Management Act hit workers in the secondary economy harder than those in the primary. The "other economy" is rife with small, unstable, fly-by-night firms, employing a high percentage of women and minorities—a combination of circumstances that makes unionization difficult. When, in addition, the law is weighted against labor (as it has come to be), the organization of people in the lesser economy is painfully difficult, adding still another wedge to widen the growing gap between the two economies. Labor law reform that would simply restore the spirit of the original Wagner Act would help the battle of those in the nether economy to stay abreast.

### A Social Wage

To introduce a measure of greater equity between earnings in the two economies, there should be a continuance and extension of all those measures that supplement the traditional wage with a "social wage." By "social wage," we refer to rent supplements, medicare and medicaid, food stamps, low-income subsidized housing, health care, social security, and the like.

This social wage has, in our lifetime, made a profound difference in the lives of the poor in America. According to a Congressional Budget Office study of January 1977 (*Poverty Status of Families Under Alternative Definitions of Income*), if income were based solely on straight earnings more than one-quarter of the nation's families would be living in poverty as officially defined. When the various kinds of "social wage" are added—whether in cash or in kind—the number of families living in poverty falls to 11.4 percent.

A social wage is a way to introduce a modicum of justice in society's reward to workers who, despite their contributions to the society, are paid much less than other workers in more fortunate sectors of the economy.

### Mandatory Controls

In a period of inflation, it is necessary to impose price controls— mandatory controls—on wages, prices, and every other aspect of the economy amenable to such regulation. Such controls are an immediate must, even as we work toward longer-range policies to get at the root causes of inflation.

The above measures are, by no means, a complete catalog of potential remedies. There are other—perhaps more basic—proposals on how to elevate the earnings of women in the economy. If we really decided to develop supplementary (alternative) sources of energy and decided to do so with the "moral equivalent of war," we would certainly find a great shortage of workers in the construction trades—to erect solar, wind, tidal, biomass, geothermal, etc., facilities. World War II's Rosie the Riveter would now become Sarah the Solar Installer. Women's wages would leap dramatically.

Should we move—as we are very likely to do—toward mandatory controls, wage guidelines could be set on a dollar-and-cents, rather than on a percentage, basis. Percentage guidelines advantage the already advantaged; fixed quantitative guidelines help narrow the gap between top and bottom. Still another strategy might consider subsidies to businesses (usually small) in the competitive sector. Present subsidies to big business are so common that to extend the generosity to lesser entrepreneurs should hardly violate any sacred principles. The subsidy might indeed go directly toward paying wages.

I offer these several suggestions because I believe it important that the work of our committee should not be considered to have ended in a *cul de sac*. We have pointed out the degree of the problem; we have probed the causes; we have wisely noted that there is no easy solution through a technical fix; we have appraised the value of job evaluation systems in specific circumstances. What I have tried to do is to argue that there are ways to cope with the problem—ways that may not properly be before a committee of "scientists" but that are most appropriately before that committee of the whole known as the electorate.

# Minority Report

ERNEST J. MCCORMICK[1]

The report of the Committee on Occupational Classification and Analysis deals generally with the issue of alleged discrimination in pay in the form of inequitable treatment based on sex or race. In connection with the report there are two issues with which I am in disagreement and that make it impossible for me to concur with portions of the report. Because of my disagreement on these issues I am writing this minority report.

Before setting forth the bases of these disagreements, I would like to refer to the composition of the committee, with particular reference to

[1] Professional background especially relevant to committee activities. Work experience: chief, planning unit, occupational research program, U.S. Employment Service, 1935–1939; chief occupational analyst, population census, Bureau of the Census, 1939–1941; chief, occupational statistics, Selective Service System, 1941–1943; personnel classification officer, U.S. Navy, 1943–1945; professor of industrial psychology, Purdue University (including primary research activities for 20 years in job analysis and teaching courses in job analysis), 1948–1977. Relevant publications: *Job Analysis: Methods and Applications*, American Management Associations, 1979; chapter on "Job and Task Analysis" in *Handbook of Industrial and Organizational Psychology*, M. D. Dunnette, ed., Rand McNally, 1976; chapter on "Job Information: Its Development and Applications" in *ASPA Handbook of Personnel Relations*, D. Yoder and H. H. Heneman, Jr., eds., Bureau of National Affairs, 1974; chapters on "Job and Task Analysis" and "Job Evaluation" in *Industrial Engineering Handbook*, G. Salvendy, ed., John Wiley & Sons (in press); 36 technical reports dealing with job analysis and job evaluation; 5 chapters in technical reports dealing with job analysis; several papers in professional journals. Other: consultant on job analysis to the U.S. Employment Service; leader in job analysis workshops. Currently: professor emeritus, Purdue University; 1315 Sunset Lane, West Lafayette, Indiana 47906.

the topical domain with which it dealt, namely, the matter of procedures for establishing equitable pay rates for jobs, which can involve the processes of job evaluation. The report of any committee that deals with a controversial subject typically reflects the composition of the committee. In the case of this committee there was no member who was a full-time practitioner in the field of job evaluation, and only a very few members had had any specific experience with, or involvement with, practical job evaluation procedures or with the job analysis processes that are basic to job evaluation and wage determination. The original committee appointments did include an industrial engineer who was deeply involved in job evaluation processes as a consultant, but he resigned shortly after the committee was formed because of possible conflict of interests. I recommended that a person with his background and experience be appointed to replace him, but this was not done. [Biographical sketches of committee members and staff appear at the end of the volume.]

Neither was there anyone on the staff who, to my knowledge, had had practical experience in the field of job evaluation. Furthermore, most of the members of the staff had had no experience in the occupational field as broadly conceived, including exposure to job evaluation and its underlying job analysis processes. I believe the activities of the committee were influenced by (and in my opinion seriously impaired because of) the very limited representation on the committee and staff of persons with familiarity with, or practical experiences in, job evaluation processes and the underlying field of job analysis.

### Criterion for Determining Job Values

One of the critical issues of this minority statement relates to the standard or the criterion that should be used in judging the "worth" of jobs. Before discussing such standards, however, it would be appropriate to differentiate between two frames of reference in which alleged discrimination is discussed. One frame of reference concerns the matter of "equal pay for equal work," which deals with pay for jobs that are the same or very similar in content. The other reference point concerns the concept of equal pay for "comparable" work or work of "comparable worth" or "comparable" or "equal value." (The committee report deals largely with the "comparable worth" frame of reference.)

The Equal Pay Act of 1963 and Title VII of the Civil Rights Act of 1964 both provide for equal pay for equal work and state that it is discriminatory for men and women performing equal work to be paid differently. On legal and rational grounds there is no justification for such discrimination. The report of the committee strongly supports the objectives of ensuring equal pay for equal work as construed in the frame of reference of equal pay for jobs that are similar in content, and I fully concur in the portions of the report that deal with this concept. My concern deals primarily with the question of the standards or criteria that might be relevant for evaluating the "comparability" of jobs.

The committee report is sprinkled with direct references or implications relating to alleged discrimination in the case of certain jobs in which women tend to dominate (these are sometimes called "women's jobs") as contrasted with those in which men tend to dominate (these are sometimes called "men's jobs"). It is alleged that the pay scales for some women's jobs are lower than they "should be," and that such rates are as low as they are because employment in them is dominated by women. Such alleged discrimination is sometimes referred to as institutional discrimination, the theory being that cultural and other factors have resulted in the "tracking" of women into such jobs, with accompanying pay scales below what they "should be." The argument that differences in the pay of women's jobs and men's jobs reflect a form of discrimination has given rise to the concept of equal pay for comparable work (or for work of comparable value or equal value), the implication being that there is some concept of comparability of jobs that would make it possible to justify the establishment of equal pay for jobs that are different in content but comparable in terms of the concept of worth or value. This argument immediately raises the question as to the basis on which jobs might be considered comparable in worth (or noncomparable).

In the report of the committee there are numerous statements that either directly, or by implication or inference, take issue with the principle that the prevailing rates of pay in the labor market should serve as the primary basis for the establishment of pay scales for jobs in specific situations. Furthermore, the committee report implies that the determination of the comparability in worth between jobs should be independent of current wages and salaries found in the labor market. It is with these portions of the report that I am in disagreement, since it is my firm conviction that current wages and salaries are indeed one indication of the underlying relationship between jobs. This relationship between worth and pay, albeit imperfect, is a product of real, impartial forces (as well as of the various possible biases that trouble the committee) and thus cannot rationally be ignored.

It is my contention that there is no conceptually appropriate, economically viable, or practical basis for determining the comparability of jobs without considering the value system that underlies the wages and salaries paid to all jobs throughout the entire occupational structure of our economy. Stated differently, I am convinced that the comparable worth or value as reflected in the going rates of pay assigned to jobs will over time closely correlate with the underlying hierarchy of values that has evolved in our world of work. This hierarchy of values generally reflects the fact that job values are influenced by a variety of factors such as skill, effort, responsibility, type of work activity, and working conditions. Furthermore, this value system is essentially a function of the supply of, and the demand for, individuals who possess the relevant job skills, who have the ability to apply the relevant effort, who are capable of assuming the relevant responsibilities, who can perform the work activities in question, and who are able and willing to work under the working conditions in question. To ignore the value system because it does not produce results that fit certain preconceptions of job worth (whether for or against any class) reflects, in my opinion, a biased frame of reference.

The committee report views the labor market as one that tends to undervalue "women's jobs" relative to "men's jobs" and concludes that the market is discriminatory and therefore should be disregarded in establishing rates of pay. Such a view of the labor market seems to me to be naive and unrealistic. The labor market is the generic term for a value system rooted in the hierarchy of skills, effort, responsibility, and work activities (and to some extent working conditions) that comprise jobs, and the supply and demand forces that operate as organizations and workers compete in our economy. As a matter of interest, statements of female or minority "undervaluation" seem to be based upon the concept that there is a value system but that some types of individuals in certain jobs are not paid according to the underlying system. If there is no available hierarchy of worth, there is no objective basis upon which to make claims of bias. Accordingly, I am convinced that the labor market must be the arbiter of basic rates of pay and that there is no other logical, economic, or practical basis for determining the values of jobs, be it in terms of "equal" or "comparable" worth.

There are two general approaches that an organization can follow in relating pay scales for its jobs to those of corresponding jobs in the labor market. In the first place, if the jobs in question have identical counterparts in the labor market, the prevailing pay rates (or pay ranges) can be used directly for setting pay scales within the organization. In the second place, an organization can use some type of job evaluation system for setting the compensation rates for its jobs.[2] The most effective

---

[2] The committee's interim report (Treiman, 1979) provided an extensive discussion of job evaluation, and I will not discuss the process of job evaluation in this minority report.

job evaluation system usually is one that accurately examines the content of jobs (skills, effort, responsibilities, activities, working conditions, etc.) and yields relative job values (usually point values) that correspond closely with (i.e., are correlated with) prevailing rates in the labor market. In effect this means that job evaluation systems (or the procedures for deriving relative job values) should be based on, or related to, those job characteristics that gave rise to prevailing market values. To develop a job evaluation system that did not first examine (and compare) the content of jobs and, second, relate the job content to a value system that underlies our entire economy is not realistic, practical, or economically or socially desirable.

## The Use of Structured Job Analysis Procedures

The other point that underlies the preparation of this minority report is clearly related to the matter of determining the "comparability" of jobs either to determine their equality (or inequality) or to determine their comparability in the framework of "comparable worth." Such comparisons are basic to the processes of resolving questions about the equity of pay at various levels at which such questions might be raised, such as within an organization, when a complaint is brought to the attention of a regulatory agency or in the courts of law.

In this regard the committee lamented the problems of making such comparisons but chose to virtually ignore the very substantial amount of research and experience over more than two decades relating to the systematic, quantitative analysis of human work that has been demonstrated to be of substantial value in making comparisons for many types of jobs. The most directly relevant research and experience deals with what usually are called structured job analysis procedures. Actually, the committee did include a passing, very cursory reference (in Chapter 4) to such procedures in saying: "Moreover, methods of systematic job analysis, such as structured job analysis and task analysis, ought to be explored for their applicability to job evaluation—in particular, the job component method of job evaluation (McCormick and Ilgen, 1980:Ch. 18), which uses structured job analysis." Not only has the committee chosen to ignore structured job analysis procedures as they have direct relevance to the issue of comparability, but they also have failed to recognized the importance of such procedures to the fundamentals of job analysis per se, which is the foundation for all job evaluation systems.

The committee report has alluded to the role that job analysis serves in the job evaluation process. Actually, job analysis can be the Achilles' heel of any job evaluation technique. Clearly, the impact of unreliable, invalid, and biased job analysis information on the job evaluation process could lead to an "unfair" pay plan. Again, the committee failed to acknowledge the value of structured job analysis procedures in the realm of job analysis in general and specifically in the application of such procedures to job evaluation. The bibliography to this minority report includes a limited sample of some of the research literature regarding the systematic analysis of human work, particularly that relating to structured job analysis procedures. Many of these listed works clearly demonstrate the practical utility of structured job analysis procedures and support the contention that, for certain purposes—such as comparing jobs with each other in quantitative terms—such procedures are superior to conventional verbal descriptions. Several researchers have clearly shown how data obtained with structured job analysis questionnaires can be used for such key personnel administrative functions as job evaluation.

Structured job analysis procedures have two possible applications that are directly relevant to the interests of the committee, these two applications being closely related. One application deals with the actual comparison of jobs in terms of similarities and differences, and the other deals with establishing pay rates for jobs that would minimize possible differentials based on sex or race. Basically, structured job analysis procedures provide for the documentation of the content of jobs in terms of a set of job elements. These elements typically are descriptive of work tasks ("job-oriented" elements) or of basic human job behaviors ("worker-oriented" elements) and are listed together in a job analysis questionnaire. In the analysis of jobs with such a questionnaire, the person making the analysis rates each element in terms of its relevance to the job, or, in certain instances, simply indicates whether the element does or does not apply to the job. (The reader interested in a further explanation of the nature of structured job analysis questionnaires is referred to Appendix A.)

As indicated previously, one relevant application of structured job analysis procedures is that of comparing jobs in terms of their similarities and differences. At a simple job-to-job level, two or more jobs can be compared even by a visual review of the ratings given to the jobs on the various job elements being used, as illustrated by the following hypothetical example:

| Job Element | Job A | Job B | Job C | Job D |
|---|---|---|---|---|
| *a* | 1 | 1 | 1 | 3 |
| *b* | 4 | 4 | 3 | 1 |
| *c* | 0 | 0 | 0 | 2 |
| *d* | 3 | 3 | 3 | 0 |
| — | — | — | — | — |
| *n* | 2 | 2 | 2 | 4 |

NOTE: Ratings: 0 = low; 5 = high.

Jobs A and B are identical, job C is almost the same as jobs A and B, but job D differs markedly from the other three. The fact that data for the job elements are quantified makes it possible to compare jobs in quantitative terms. Most typically, some statistical index of similarity is derived for each pair of jobs. In turn, such indexes frequently are used for grouping jobs into groups that have reasonably similar profiles of job element values. In the use of task inventories in the U.S. Air Force, for example, such procedures are used to identify "job types," that is, groups of positions that are reasonably similar in the combinations of tasks that are performed (Christal, 1974). As another example, Taylor and Colbert (1978) obtained data with a "worker-oriented" type of structured job analysis questionnaire used to study jobs in an insurance company, and they found 13 job families, each family being characterized by a group of jobs with very similar behavioral components.

The possibility of being able to use statistical procedures for comparing positions or jobs in terms of their similarities, and of grouping them into job types or job families, would seem to be substantially relevant in instances of possible discrimination. In this regard the use of job-oriented questionnaires (task inventories) would be most appropriate in connection with the equal work concept if "equal work" is viewed in the framework of the specific tasks of the positions or jobs in question. If the equal work concept were interpreted as embracing similarities in the basic human behaviors involved in jobs, however, the worker-oriented type of structured job analysis questionnaire would be appropriate.

The second possible application of data from structured job analysis questionnaires that would be relevant to the charge of the committee is with regard to their use in job evaluation. Their use for this purpose is distinctly different from conventional job evaluation methods in that the judgmental evaluation process is eliminated, the job values being derived statistically. Such a procedure is called the job component job evaluation method (Jeanneret, 1980; McCormick, 1979:317–21; McCormick and Ilgen, 1980:375–78). The procedure as typically carried out involves the following steps:

1. The analysis of a sample of jobs in terms of an appropriate structured job analysis questionnaire with job elements consisting of tasks or basic human behaviors, and usually working conditions. The individual job elements, or statistically related groups thereof, can be considered as job components.

2. The derivation, for this sample of jobs, of money values for the individual components, in particular indexes of the extent to which the individual components contribute to the going rates of pay for the jobs. (This is a statistical procedure.)

3. The analysis with the structured job analysis questionnaire of specific jobs for which evaluations are to be made.

4. The derivation of an index of the total monetary value for each such job. This is done by "building up" the total value for each job from the indexes of the relevance of the individual components to the job, in combination with the money values of the components as previously derived from the original sample of jobs as described in steps 1 and 2. (A more specific description of the job component method of job evaluation can be found in Appendix B.)

In line with the comments made earlier, if the concept of equal work is interpreted in terms of specific work activities such as tasks, the job-oriented type of questionnaire (a task inventory) would be required in the job component method of job evaluation. Certain applications of this approach serve as illustrations, such as the study by Miles (1952) in the case of office jobs and the study by Tornow and Pinto (1976) in the case of managerial jobs. A variation of this general approach is suggested by Christal (1974).

If the concept of equal work were interpreted as applying to the similarity of basic human behaviors in jobs (as contrasted to work tasks), the worker-oriented type of structured questionnaire would be relevant. In this regard, for example, Jeanneret (1972) used such a questionnaire to place various utility company jobs in several pay grades and then compared the average actual pay of men and women in each of the "new" pay grades. In this instance he found a salary difference of $108 a month in favor of men. In studies completed for another utility company and for a savings and loan organization, similar comparisons also revealed appreciable salary differences (Jeanneret, 1978). (In these companies the salaries of women were subsequently adjusted.) The general indication from such studies is that a worker-oriented type of structured job analysis questionnaire can, as Jeanneret (1978) expresses it, "document the content of jobs without regard to sex of the incumbents . . . and fairly evaluate jobs without regard to the sex of the incumbents."

If the objective of a job evaluation plan is to derive estimates of equal pay for comparable work (as opposed to equal pay for equal work) the worker-oriented type of structured job analysis questionnaire definitely would be the more appropriate. Thus, it is believed that such structured job analysis questionnaires could serve as the basis for determining the "comparability" of jobs if ultimately the law or the courts would provide the basis for "equal pay for comparable work" as contrasted with "equal pay for equal work."

In summary, I would like to emphasize the point that there have been significant developments in the past couple of decades in the development and use of systematic methods of analysis of human work and in the use of such methods for various practical purposes such as the quantitative comparison of jobs with each other, the identification of job types or job families, and job evaluation. There seems to be no question but that the nature and scope of these developments have substantial potential relevance to the objectives of the committee. In view of this I feel that the committee report is seriously deficient since it refers to such work with only a casual one-sentence comment. In my opinion the failure of the committee to include more adequate discussion of structured job analysis procedures reflects the fact that the staff and most members of the committee were not sufficiently familiar with the developments in this area over the past couple of decades and therefore failed to appreciate the possible relevance of such procedures to the objectives of the committee.

The two issues raised in this minority report would seem to be compatible with each other. The job component method of job evaluation is of course based on the use of going rates of pay as the standard or criterion for determining the money values of various types of work behaviors, but at the same time the use of structured job analysis procedures in this process seems to make it possible to "document the content of jobs without regard to sex of the incumbent . . . and fairly evaluate jobs without regard to sex of the incumbents" (Jeanneret, 1978).

## APPENDIX A: STRUCTURED JOB ANALYSIS QUESTIONNAIRES

A structured job analysis questionnaire consists of a specific list of job elements that can be used in the analysis of jobs. There are various types of job elements that can be used in structured job analysis procedures, although there are two types that are particularly relevant. In the first place, some structured job analysis questionnaires, commonly called task inventories, provide for the analysis of jobs in terms of each of a number of tasks that might be performed by individuals within a given occupational area. Examples of such occupational areas are health services, office operations, automobile mechanics, and engineering. Examples of tasks that might be included in task inventories are: types straight copy from rough draft; removes and replaces spark plugs; takes orders for meals from customers; and estimates costs of building materials from building plans and specifications. Task inventories have been referred to as "job-oriented" questionnaires in that they provide for describing jobs in terms of the output or end-result of tasks. In the usual task inventory it is typically the practice for the job incumbent to indicate, for each task, whether he or she performs the task or not, and in addition, to indicate something about the degree of involvement with each task, such as the frequency of performance or the time spent on the task.

Task inventories frequently are used as the basis for identifying "job types" that consist of jobs or positions with relatively similar combinations of tasks. This sometimes is carried out with a hierarchical grouping technique that involves the derivation of a statistical index of the degree of similarity of the tasks performed for every possible pair of jobs or positions in the sample being used. Such statistical indexes conceivably could be relevant in comparing the similarity of jobs about which some discrimination issue has been raised. Furthermore, the possibility of identifying job types by statistical procedures might also have some relevance in connection with charges relating to discrimination.

It should be pointed out that the use of any given task inventory would be restricted to the specific occupational area for which it was prepared. It is expected that there are certain types of occupational areas for which task inventories might not be feasible.

The second type of structured job analysis questionnaire provides for the analysis of jobs in terms of more generalized, basic human job behaviors that transcend or cut across occupational areas. Such questionnaires are referred to as "worker-oriented" questionnaires in that they provide for analyzing jobs in terms that describe, or imply, the basic human behaviors involved in work activities. One such questionnaire, reported by McCormick (1979, pp. 147–49) and McCormick, Jeanneret, and Mecham (1972) provides for analyzing jobs in terms of each of 187 job elements. Some examples (in paraphrased form) are: uses visual displays (as a source of job information); uses measuring devices; arranges or positions objects in a specific position or arrangement; operates keyboard devices; conducts interviews with others; works under high-temperature conditions. In the analysis of a job with this questionnaire the analyst uses an appropriate rating scale to indicate the involvement of the job incumbent with each job element. Various types of rating scales are used, such as the degree of importance, the amount of time involved, the "extent of use" of various kinds of materials, and so forth.

This particular questionnaire has been subjected to a form of factor analysis (specifically, principal components analysis) that identifies the job elements that tend to "go together" in jobs and that form what are called job dimensions. Each such job dimension can be thought of as being based primarily on the group of job elements that tend to occur in common across jobs in general. Some examples of job dimensions are: interpreting what is sensed; processing information; performing handling and related activities; exchanging job-related information; being alert to changing conditions; and potentially hazardous situations. Collectively, these job dimensions can be viewed as reflecting the "structure" of human work in terms of the basic types of human behavior that are involved in work activities. With the analysis of a job using the structured job analysis questionnaire in question it is possible to derive a score for the job on each dimension. Such scores represent a "profile" for the job, and can be used as quantitative indexes of the dimensions.

## APPENDIX B: THE JOB COMPONENT METHOD OF JOB EVALUATION

The job component method of job evaluation is based on the use of a structured job analysis questionnaire in the analysis of jobs. There are various ways in which data from such questionnaires can be used in the derivation of money values of jobs, but the basic procedure referred to earlier is the one dealt with in this appendix. In actual use in deriving indexes of job values the method involves two steps. In the first place the jobs are analyzed with the structured job analysis questionnaire being used. In the second place a statistical equation is used to derive an index of the total value for each job. The equation incorporates a weight for each job "component." The job components may be individual job elements, or combinations of elements based on factor analysis, the factors usually being called job dimensions. In deriving a total value for a job the "weight" for each component is multiplied by the value of that component for the job, resulting in an arithmetic "product," for each component. These products for all components are then added together to derive a total value for the job.

The central basis for the job component method of job evaluation is in the derivation of the weights for the individual components. For this purpose data for a sample of jobs are used. Each job is analyzed with the structured job analysis questionnaire, producing a value for each component for each job. In addition, information on the rate of pay for each job is obtained. Regression analysis is then used for the total sample to determine the statistical contribution of each component to the rates of pay for the jobs in the sample. From this analysis it is possible to derive the appropriate weight for each component. These weights can be thought of as reflecting the money "values" of the individual components in the labor market; that is, how much the individual components are "worth" in the labor market. If, collectively, data on the "values" of the job components of a structured job analysis questionnaire predict going rates of pay with acceptable accuracy for a sample of jobs, these money values can then be used as the basis for the estimation of total rates of pay for other jobs.

In a sense, then, the central objective of the job component method of job evaluation is to develop regression equations that, by and large, reflect the approximate contributions of different job components to the market values of jobs. In the operational use of this method a regression equation based on a broad, varied sample of jobs from various industries and geographical areas has been found to be reasonably applicable in various situations. However, it would be expected that, in the long run, the derivation of job values would be more accurate if the money values of the various job components were derived from data on samples of jobs of different major types and within particular labor market areas.

Although the job component method of job evaluation has not as yet been used extensively, research and experience with it offer substantive evidence that could be used in many situations to provide the basis for the establishment of equitable rates of pay for jobs.


## BIBLIOGRAPHY

Archer, W. B. Computation of group job descriptions from occupational survey data. USAF, Personnel Research Laboratory, PRL-TR-66-12, 1966.

Archer, W. B. and Fruchter, D. A. The construction, review, and administration of Air Force job inventories. USAF, Personnel Research Laboratory, Technical Documentary Report No. 63-21, 1963.

Arvey, R. D. and Mossholder, K. V. A proposed methodology for determining similarities and differences among jobs. *Personnel Psychology*, 1977, *30*, 363–73.

Arvey, R. D., Passino, E. M. and Lounsbury, J. W. Job analysis results as influenced by sex of incumbent and sex of analyst. *Journal of Applied Psychology*, 1977, *62*, 411–16.

Baehr, M. E. A factorial framework for job descriptions for higher-level personnel. Industrial Relations Center, The University of Chicago, 1967.

Boese, R. R. and Cunningham, J. W. Systematically derived dimensions of human work. Center for Occupational Education, North Carolina State University, 1975.

Brumback, G. B., Romashko, T., Hahn, C. P. and Fleishman, E. A. Model Procedures for Job Analysis, Test Development and Validation, City of New York, Department of Personnel, July 1974.

Brumback, G. B. and Vincent, J. W. Factor analysis of work-performed data for a sample of administrative, professional, and scientific positions. *Personnel Psychology*, 1970, 23, 101–07.

Carr, M. J. The Samoa method of determining technical, organizational, and communicational dimensions of task clusters. USN, Naval Personnel Research Activity, Technical Bulletin STB 68-5, 1967.

Center for Vocational Education, The Ohio State University. Directory of task inventories (Volumes 1, 2, and 3).

Christal, R. E. Stability of consolidated job descriptions based on task inventory survey information. USAF, Personnel Research Division, Air Force Systems Command, AFHRL-TR-71-48, 1971.

Christal, R. E. New directions in the Air Force occupational research program. USAF, Personnel Research Division, AFHRL, 1972.

Christal, R. E. The United States Air Force occupational research project. USAF, Air Force Systems Command, Brooks Air Force Base, Texas, January 1974.

Cragun, J. R. and McCormick, E. J. Job inventory information: task and scale reliabilities and scale interrelationships. USAF, Personnel Research Laboratory, PRL-TR-67-15, 1967.

Cunningham, J. W. An S-O-R approach to the study of job commonalities relevant to occupational education. Center for Occupational Education, North Carolina State University, 1968.

Cunningham, J. W. The job-cluster concept and its curricular implications. Center for Occupational Education, Center Monograph No. 4, North Carolina State University, 1969.

Cunningham, J. W., Tuttle, T. C., Floyd, J. R. and Bates, J. A. The development of the Occupation Analysis Inventory: an "ergometric" approach to an educational problem. Center for Occupational Education, Center Research Monograph No. 6, North Carolina State University, 1971.

Farina, A. J., Jr. Development of a taxonomy of human performance: a review of descriptive schemes for human task behavior. American Institutes for Research, Technical Report No. 2, 1969.

Farina, A. J. and Wheaton, G. R. Development of a taxonomy of human performance: The task characteristics approach to performance prediction. American Institutes for Research, Technical Report No. 7, 1971.

Farrell, W. T. Hierarchical clustering: A bibliography. Evaluation of the Marine Corps task analysis program. California State University, Los Angeles, July 1975.

Farrell, W. T., Stone, C. H. and Yoder, D. Guidelines for research planning and design in task analysis, Technical Report No. 4, Evaluation of the Marine Corps Task Analysis Program. California State University, Los Angeles, September 1975.

Fine, S. A. Functional Job Analysis Scales: A Desk Aid. W. E. Upjohn Institute for Employment Research, Kalamazoo, Mich., April 1973.

Fleishman, E. A. Development of a behavior taxonomy for describing human tasks: a correlational-experimental approach. American Institutes for Research, 1966.

Fugill, J. W. K. Task difficulty and task aptitude benchmark scales for the mechanical and electronics career fields. USAF, Air Force Systems Command, Brooks Air Force Base, Texas, April 1972.

Gilbert, A. C. F. Dimensions of certain army officer positions derived by factor analysis. U.S. Army Research Institute for the Behavioral and Social Sciences, December 1975.

Gragg, D. B. Identification of logistics officer job type groups. USAF, AFHRL-70-39, 1970.

Gragg, D. B. An occupational survey of an airman career ladder: supply warehousing-inspection. USAF, Personnel Research Laboratory, Technical Report No. 62-19, 1962.

Hemphill, J. K. Describing managerial work. The Conference on the Executive Study. Educational Testing Service, 1961.

Hemphill, J. K. Job descriptions for executives. *Harvard Business Review*, 1959, *37*, pp. 53–67.

Jeanneret, P. R. Personal communication, 1978.

Jeanneret, P. R. Equitable job evaluation and classification with the Position Analysis Questionnaire. *Compensation Review*, First Quarter, 1980, pp. 32–42. AMACOM, American Management Associations.

Lecznar, W. B. Three methods for estimating difficulty of job tasks. USAF, AFHRL-TR-71-30, July 1971.

Levine, J. M., Romashko, T. and Fleishman, E. A. Development of a taxonomy of human performance: evaluation of an abilities classification system for integrating and generalizing research findings. American Institutes for Research, Technical Report No. 12, 1971.

McCormick, E. J. *Job Analysis: Methods and Applications*. New York: AMACOM, American Management Associations, 1979.

McCormick, E. J. and Ilgen, D. R. *Industrial Psychology* (7th ed.). Englewood Cliffs, New Jersey, 1980.

McCormick, E. J., Jeanneret, P. R. and Mecham, R. C. A study of job characteristics and job dimensions as based on the Position Analysis Questionnaire (PAQ). *Journal of Applied Psychology*, 1972, 56, 347–68.

Mayo, C. C. A method for determining job types for low aptitude airmen. USAF, AFHRL-TR-69-35, 1969.

Mead, D. F. and Christal, R. E. Development of a constant standard weight equation for evaluating job difficulty. USAF, AFHRL-TR-70-44, 1970.

Mead, D. F. Development of an equation for evaluating job difficulty. USAF, AFHRL-TR-70-42, 1970.

Mecham, R. C. and McCormick, E. J. The use in job evaluation of job elements and job dimensions based on the Position Analysis Questionnaire. Psychology Department, Purdue University, Report No. 3, 1969.

Melching, H. W. and Boucher, S. D. Procedures for constructing and using Task Inventories. Center for Vocational and Technical Education, The Ohio State University, Research and Development Series No. 91, 1973.

Miles, M. C. Studies in job evaluation: a. Validity of a check list for evaluating office jobs. *Journal of Applied Psychology*, 1952, *36*, 97–101.

Morsh, J. E. Analyzing work behavior. A paper presented at the American Psychological Association, 1963.

Morsh, J. E. Evolution of a job inventory and tryout of task rating factors. USAF, Personnel Research Laboratory, Technical Report No. 65-22, 1965.

Morsh, J. E. Identification of job types in the personnel career field. USAF, Personnel Research Laboratory, Technical Report No.65-9, 1965.

Morsh, J. E. Job types identified with an inventory constructed by Telectronics engineers. USAF, Personnel Research Laboratory, Technical Report No. 66-6, 1966.

Morsh, J. E. and Archer, W. B. Procedural guide for conducting occupational surveys in the United States Air Force. USAF, Personnel Research Laboratory, Technical Report 67-11, 1967.

Morsh, J. E. and Christal, R. E. Impact of the computer on job analysis in the United States Air Force. USAF, Personnel Research Laboratory, Technical Report 66-19, 1966.

Pass, J. J. and Cunningham, J. W. A systematic procedure for estimating the attribute requirements of occupations. Report No. 11 of the Ergometric Research and Development Series. Center for Occupational Education, North Carolina State University, 1975.

Riccobono, J. A. and Cunningham, J. W. Work dimensions derived through systematic job analysis: a study of the Occupation Analysis Inventory. Center for Occupational Education, Center Research Monograph No. 8, North Carolina State University, 1971.

Riccobono, J. A. and Cunningham, J. W. Work dimensions derived through systematic job analysis: a replicated study of the Occupation Analysis Inventory. Center for Occupational Education, Center Research Monograph No. 9, North Carolina State University, 1971.

Riccobono, J. A., Cunningham, J. W. and Boese, R. R. Clusters of occupations based on systematically derived work dimensions: an exploratory study. Report No. 10 of the Ergometric Research and Development Series. Center for Occupational Education, North Carolina State University, 1974.

Silverman, J. A computer technique for clustering tasks. USN, Naval Personnel Research Activity, Technical Bulletin STB 66-23, 1966.

Silverman, J. New techniques in task analysis. USN, Naval Personnel Research Activity, Research Memorandum No. SRM 68-12, 1967.

Sprecher, T. B. Dimensions of engineers' job performance. Educational Testing Service, Research Bulletin, 1965.

Stone, C. H. Evaluation of the Marine Corps Task Analysis Program, Technical Report No. 16. California State University, Los Angeles, June 1976.

Taylor, L. R. and Colbert, G. A. Empirically derived job families as a foundation for the study of validity generalization: Study II. The construction of job families based on company-specific PAQ job dimensions. *Personnel Psychology*, 1978, *31*, 341–55.

Teichner, W. H. and Whitehead, J. Development of a taxonomy of human performance: Evaluation of a task classification system for generalizing research findings from a data base. American Institutes for Research, Technical Report 8, April 1971.

Tornow, W. W. and Pinto, P. R. The development of a managerial job taxonomy: A system for describing, classifying, and evaluating executive positions. *Journal of Applied Psychology*, 1976, *61*, 410–18.

Treiman, Donald. *Job Evaluation: An Analytic Review.* Interim Report to the Equal Employment Opportunity Commission. Committee on Occupational Classification and Analysis, National Research Council. Washington, D.C.: National Academy of Sciences, 1979.

Tuttle, T. C. and Cunningham, J. W. Affective correlates of systematically derived work dimensions: Validation of the Occupation Analysis Inventory. Ergometric research and development series, Report No. 7. Center research monograph No. 10. Center for Occupational Education. North Carolina State University, 1972.

U.S. Department of Health, Education, and Welfare. Major tasks and knowledge clusters involved in performance of electronic technicians' work, 1966.

U.S. Air Force, Personnel Research Division, AFHRL. Proceedings of Division 19 of the American Psychological Association. Division of Military Psychology Symposium: Collecting, analyzing, and reporting information describing jobs and occupations, 1969.

U.S. Department of Labor, Manpower Administration. Task analysis inventories: A method for collecting job information, 1973.

Wheaton, G. R. Development of a taxonomy of human performance: a review of classificatory systems relating to tasks and performance. American Institute for Research, Technical Report 1, 1968.

Wiley, L. N., Jenkins, S. and Cagwin, L. P. Job types of communications officers, USAF, Personnel Research Laboratory, Technical Report No. 66-17, 1966.

# Biographical Sketches
of Committee Members
and Staff

ANN R. MILLER is professor of sociology at the University of Pennsylvania and a senior research associate at its Population Studies Center. She was formerly a consultant to the Office of Management and Budget on occupational classification and analysis and has served on several advisory committees of the National Institute of Child Health and Human Development and the Bureau of the Census. Her research has been primarily in the fields of labor force, occupational, and geographic mobility. She is a fellow of the American Statistical Association and a member of the Population Association of America and the Economic History Association. She received an AB from Bryn Mawr College and a PhD from the University of Pennsylvania.

DAVID P. CAMPBELL is executive vice president of the Center for Creative Leadership in Greensboro, North Carolina, and adjunct professor of psychology at Duke University. Campbell received BS and MS degrees from Iowa State University and a PhD from the University of Minnesota. His professional work began in psychometrics and career development, then turned to interest measurement and the role of interests in career planning and development; he coauthored the Strong-Campbell Interest Inventory. He has recently been involved in research on leadership and creativity. He is a fellow of the Division of Industrial and Organizational Psychology, the Division on Evaluation and Measurement, and the Division of Counseling Psychology of the American Psychological Association.

MARY C. DUNLAP is a lawyer and a visiting lecturer in the Field Studies Program of the University of California, Berkeley. She is cofounder of and former teacher and staff attorney of Equal Rights Advocates, Inc., a public interest law firm specializing in litigation and clinical legal education concerning sex-based discrimination. Previously she served as a visiting assistant professor of law at the University of Texas at Austin. In 1977 she argued before the Supreme Court a case involving leave for pregnant schoolteachers. She has taught, lectured, and written widely on equality and discrimination. She received a BA in psychology and a JD from the University of California, Berkeley.

G. FRANKLIN EDWARDS is professor and former head of the Department of Sociology at Howard University. His major professional interests are the study of minorities in professional and other white-collar occupations and race relations. He has been a member of various government panels concerned with training programs for manpower development. He is a member of the American Sociological Association. He received an AB from Fisk University and a PhD from the University of Chicago.

RICHARD C. EDWARDS is associate professor of economics at the University of Massachusetts at Amherst. He has held positions with the National Bureau of Economic Research and the Harvard Graduate School of Education. His work focuses on American economic development, including the political economy of industrial organization and labor relations. He received a BA from Grinnell College and a PhD from Harvard University.

LEON FESTINGER is Staudinger professor of social psychology at the New School for Social Research. He has a BS from City College of New York and MA and PhD degrees from the University of Iowa. He received the American Psychological Association's distinguished scientist award in 1959 for his work on the theory of cognitive dissonance. His research interests have included cognitive theory and statistics and research methods as well as vision and, more recently, archaeology. He is a member of the National Academy of Sciences and the American Association for the Advancement of Science; he is a fellow of the American Psychological Association and the American Academy of Arts and Sciences.

GARY D. GOTTFREDSON is a research scientist and director of the Program in Delinquency and School Environments at the Center for Social Organization of Schools of the Johns Hopkins University, where he is also assistant professor of psychology and of social relations. He received a PhD in psychology from Johns Hopkins in 1976. Formerly he was associate administrative officer at the American Psychological Association. He has published on the measurement of vocational interests and the career development of men and women, and he is now doing research on school organizational forms and delinquency prevention.

JOHN A. HARTIGAN is professor of statistics at Yale University. Previously he was professor of statistics and mathematics at Princeton University. His principal interests are the foundations of statistics and probability, classification, and statistical computing. He is a fellow of the American Statistical Association, a member of the International Statistical Institute, and past president of the Classification Society. He received a BSc and MSc from the University of Sydney and a PhD from Princeton University.

DORIS P. HAYWOOD is a vice president of Metropolitan Life Insurance Company. She works in the personnel administrative division of the company's human resources department. As head of the equal employment opportunity unit, she is responsible for the company's affirmative action programs. In the course of her 35-year career at Metropolitan, Haywood has held the positions of secretary, assistant to the personnel officer, career opportunity coordinator, manager of the equal employment opportunity unit, and assistant vice president. In 1979 she received the Achievement Award of the Women's Equity Action League for women in business and labor, and in 1977 received the Black Achievers in Industry Award from the YMCA of Greater New York and the Volunteer Service Award of the Children's Aid Society. She is a member of the Corporate Women's Network, the Life Office Management Association's EEO/Affirmative Action Committee and the Institute Council, and the EEO Working Group of the U.S. Chamber of Commerce.

WESLEY R. LIEBTAG is director of personnel programs of the International Business Machines Corporation. In that capacity, he has responsibility for the company's worldwide compensation systems. Liebtag began his career at IBM in 1946 as a marketing representative and subsequently served in a number of marketing and general management posts. Before assuming his present position in 1967, he served as director of compensation and benefits administration. He was a member of the task force of the Cost of Living Council in 1973. He was executive director of the President's Commission on Executive Compensation in 1976. He served as an adviser to the recent Council on Wage and Price

Stabilization. He is a member of the Conference Board's Council on Compensation.

ROBERT E. B. LUCAS is associate professor of economics at Boston University. He is also affiliated with the University's Center for Asian Development Studies, Center for Latin American Development Studies, and African Studies Center. Previously he was affiliated with the Institute for International Economic Studies in Stockholm and the Economics Department of the University of California, Los Angeles. He has done research on the occupational characteristics of the U.S. labor force; currently his interests include international migration studies, income distribution in Botswana, and human resources in developing countries. He has BSc and MSc degrees from the London School of Economics and a PhD from Massachusetts Institute of Technology.

KAREN OPPENHEIM MASON is associate professor of sociology and research associate of the Population Studies Center at the University of Michigan. She has held positions at the University of Wisconsin at Madison and the Research Triangle Institute in North Carolina. Her research focuses on the sociology of gender and on population studies and has included such topics as changing sex role attitudes, historical patterns of women's labor force participation, and the interrelationship between women's employment and fertility. She received a BA from Reed College and MA and PhD degrees in sociology from the University of Chicago.

ERNEST J. MCCORMICK is professor emeritus of industrial psychology at Purdue University and president of PAQ Services, Inc. Prior to his three decades at Purdue, he held various positions: chief of the planning unit, occupation research program, U.S. Employment Service; chief occupational analyst, Bureau of the Census; chief, occupational statistics, Selective Service System; personnel classification officer, U.S. Navy. From 1948 to 1977 he was a faculty member in industrial psychology at Purdue University. His research has dealt primarily with methods of job analysis, including the development of the Position Analysis Questionnare, a computerized job analysis procedure. He received the James McKeen Cattell Award of the Division of Industrial and Organizational Psychology, American Psychological Association, in 1964; the Franklin V. Taylor Award of the Society of Engineering Psychologists in 1966; and the Paul M. Fitts Award of the Human Factors Society in 1972. He has served as a member of the Army Scientific Advisory Panel, the Research and Engineering Advisory Council of the Postmaster General, and the Navy Advisory Board for Human Resources. He received MS and PhD degrees from Purdue University.

GUS TYLER is assistant president of the International Ladies' Garment Workers' Union and director of its Department of Politics, Education and Training. He received a BA from New York University. He is a senior fellow of the Aspen Institute for Humanistic Studies; national chairman of the American Veterans Committee; council member for the United States and chairman of the U.S. Council of the World Veterans Federation. He has served as lecturer or instructor at Hunter College, Adelphi University, Columbia University, the New School for Social Research, the College of the City of New York, Cornell University, Rutgers University, the University of Wisconsin, and Pennsylvania State University. He serves as a consultant to the Ford Foundation and as a board member of the Institute for the Future, the Fund for the City of New York, and WNET/Channel 13 (Educational Broadcasting Corporation). He is a member of the National Institute of Education's Vocational Education Study Consultant's Group. He writes a syndicated column and is also the author of books and articles on crime, the economy, politics, and trade unionism.

DONALD J. TREIMAN took a leave of absence from the University of California, Los Angeles, where he is professor of sociology, to serve as study director to the Committee on Occupational Classification and Analysis. He extended his stay at the National Research Council to serve as study director for the Committee on Basic Research in the Behavioral and Social Sciences, but will return to UCLA in September 1981. His academic research interests center on the comparative study of social stratification and social mobility. He has written extensively on problems of occupational classification and measurement, including a book analyzing occupational prestige data from 60 countries. He has a BA from Reed College, and MA and PhD degrees from the University of Chicago, all in sociology.

HEIDI I. HARTMANN began her association with the National Research Council as research associate for the Committee on Occupational Classification and Analysis. She has since become associate executive director of the Assembly of Behavioral and Social Sciences, National Research Council. Previously she was a member of the graduate economics faculty of the New School for Social Research and a research economist at the U.S. Commission on Civil Rights, where she directed a research project on internal labor markets and discrimination against

women and minorities. Her research interests center on employment
issues related to women and minorities. She has a BA from Swarthmore
College and M Phil and PhD degrees from Yale University, all in economics.

① even if have a measure of "worth", can still the
issue ② what to do if people sort into
jobs ② worth and a done by sex or race
— e.g. what if ♀ disproportionate in
jobs of lower worth? still problem of
just allocation

② how would defining structure on basis of
"worth" be different from present structure?
— assumption is that ♀'s work is of equal worth
so changing pay scales will reward fairly
what is already the case.